'Informative and eng[illegible] written, Rob Yeung explains why you are the way y[illegible] ow to be the best you can be.'

[illegible] inks, Partner and Managing Director, The Boston Consulting Group

'People wit[illegible] ersona[illegible] have more fulfilling careers and personal lives. This book is a g[illegible] unlocking your potential.'

Fred van der Tang, UK Manag[illegible] ector, global recruitment firm Randstad

'Presenting deep insights with simpl[illegible] you engage better with others and e[illegible]

Max Landsberg, Partner at executive se[illegible] and au[illegible]

'I'm not sure he quite realises (if he does, he's far too modest to mention it), but Rob is a miracle worker. And I don't use that term lightly.'

Malcolm Green, Head of Creative Development, Naked Communications

'Whether you are looking for a job or a promotion, going into performing arts, expecting a child, getting married, *Personality* shows you how to focus on your strengths and build a successful future.'

Felix Schachter, Head of Group Strategy, AXA UK & Ireland

'Find out who you are, where you want to be and how to get there.'

Carol-Ann White, HR Director, public relations firm LEWIS

'If you are ready to understand your own personality, make it work for you, and, as Rob puts it, "ready for success", then this book is for you.'

Steve Huxham, Chairman, The Recruitment Society

'An indispensable guide to discovering yourself and understanding how to lead others effectively.'

Richard Brady, CEO, Mentis Consulting

'One of the most insightful, practical and genuinely helpful books I have read in years.'

Sarah McNeil, Managing Director, The Admirable Crichton

'Filled with insights from one of the country's top psychologists, *Personality* is a must-read book for anyone serious about success.'

David Langdon, Director, business consultancy firm Xancam

'Rob Yeung has done it again – he has written a highly accessible and research-informed book that should interest everyone.'

Adrian Furnham, Professor of Psychology, University College London

'A great guide to help you identify your strengths and find what makes you unique.'

Sahar Hashemi, Founder of Coffee Republic

'Dr Rob Yeung is one of the country's top psychologists. Personality is an eye-opening read – full of insights into how to make the most of your natural talents.'

Melinda Messenger, TV presenter and model

'A practical and accessible guide – a must read for anyone who wants greater self awareness and future success.'

Fiona Dent, Director of Executive Education, Ashridge Business School

'An engaging guide that covers the latest findings in personality research and shows how to use them to improve career performance and quality of life.'

Robert Hogan, PhD, creator of the Hogan Personality Inventory and President, Hogan Assessment Systems

'*Personality* is an extremely useful book – a must read, if you want to know more about you!'

Professor Cary L. Cooper, CBE, Lancaster University

'Entertaining and accessible, readers will find insights into who they are and who they could be.'

Matthew Taylor, Chief Executive, Royal Society of Arts

'As an expert on leadership and career success, Dr Yeung shares the secrets of what it takes to get ahead. Buy this book.'

Joe Slavin, CEO, fish4jobs.co.uk

Personality

Prentice Hall LIFE

If life is what you make it, then making it better starts here.

What we learn today can change our lives tomorrow. It can change our goals or change our minds; open up new opportunities or simply inspire us to make a difference. That's why we have created a new breed of books that do more to help you make more of *your* life.

Whether you want more confidence or less stress, a new skill or a different perspective, we've designed *Prentice Hall Life* books to help you to make a change for the better. Together with our authors we share a commitment to bring you the brightest ideas and best ways to manage your life, work and wealth.

In these pages we hope you'll find the ideas you need for the life *you* want. Go on, help yourself.

It's what you make it

* * *

Personality

How to unleash your hidden strengths

Dr Rob Yeung

Prentice Hall Life
is an imprint of

Harlow, England • London • New York • Boston • San Francisco • Toronto • Sydney • Singapore • Hong Kong
Tokyo • Seoul • Taipei • New Delhi • Cape Town • Madrid • Mexico City • Amsterdam • Munich • Paris • Milan

PEARSON EDUCATION LIMITED

Edinburgh Gate
Harlow CM20 2JE
Tel: +44 (0)1279 623623
Fax: +44 (0)1279 431059
Website: www.pearsoned.co.uk

First published in Great Britain in 2009

ISBN: 978-0-273-72494-0

British Library Cataloguing-in-Publication Data
A catalogue record for this book is available from the British Library.

Library of Congress Cataloging-in-Publication Data
Yeung, Rob.
Personality : how to unleash your hidden strengths / Rob Yeung. -- 1st ed.
p. cm.
ISBN 978-0-273-72494-0 (pbk.)
1. Personality. 2. Success. I. Title.
BF698.Y48 2009
155.2--dc22
2009021793

The publishers would like to thank Talentspace for permission to reproduce the ladder of influence figure on page 144.

10 9 8 7 6 5 4 3 2 1
13 12 11 10 09

Typeset in 10pt IowanOldStyle by 3.
Printed and bound in Great Britain by Ashford Colour Press Ltd, Gosport, Hants

The publisher's policy is to use paper manufactured from sustainable forests.

Contents

About the author

Dr Rob Yeung is widely regarded as a top business speaker and authority on the psychology of high achievement. A director at leadership consulting firm Talentspace, he also coaches leaders and their teams to accomplish their goals.

He appears frequently on television as an expert, on programmes from CNN and ITN news to *Big Brother* and the BBC's *Working Lunch*. He presents the BBC TV series *How To Get Your Dream Job*. He has written over a dozen best-selling books and is frequently quoted in the press, including the *Financial Times* and the *Guardian* newspapers.

He uses personality tests to delve into people's minds, helping organisations to hire the right people in high-stakes situations and working with managers to improve their effectiveness. He was even invited to test the personalities of celebrities on the BBC's *Strictly Come Dancing* show.

He holds two degrees in psychology, having gained a PhD in exercise and sports psychology with a particular emphasis on motivation and peak performance. He also qualified as a personal trainer and aerobics instructor and is a chartered psychologist of the British Psychological Society.

For more information, visit: www.robyeung.com and www.talentspace.co.uk.

Acknowledgements

To my parents for giving me total freedom in pursuing opportunities that suited my personality. To Steve Cuthbertson for his perpetually supportive nature. To my Talentspace colleagues for their patience. To Bonnie Chiang for her keen observations. And to my editor Sam Jackson for giving me another chance to share the fruits of my consulting work with a broader audience.

Introduction

Why do certain people succeed?

Let's consider a few. Richard Branson, Madonna, Simon Cowell, Jordan/Katie Price, Oprah Winfrey, Steve Jobs. Love 'em or loathe 'em, you can't deny that they've succeeded in their chosen fields.

So how did they hit the big time?

Because they know who they are. They understand their personal strengths and shortcomings. None of them are all-rounded and talented in every way, but they pursue endeavours that play to what they are good at. All of them manage their weaknesses and avoid situations that expose them. Rather than treading the same, old, tired path as everyone else, they carve out their own journeys to create careers that are one of a kind.

These people understand their unique personalities and make them work for them. You can too.

Your personalised plan

Each of us is unique. We all have individual traits and characteristics that we call our personality. Some of us thrive on pressure while others hate it. Some strive to be noticed while others prefer to live comfortably in the crowd. Some of us crave harmony while others revel in confrontation.

We're all different.

And if we're all different, it follows that we need to take diverse paths to succeed. What works for me may not work for you. The actions you need to get ahead will almost certainly differ from those that your best friend, partner or teammates would need to take. Rather than tell you advice aimed at the masses, I'll help you to create a personalised development programme that is specifically tailored to you and your personality.

The science of success

In this book I present you with advice that is *proven* to be effective.

I'm sure you've heard of – or even completed – personality tests. The truth is that a lot of the personality or psychometric tests out there are actually decades old. If I asked you to name a personality test, I bet I could guess which one you're thinking of. But you may be surprised to hear that it was probably developed over 50 years ago. Psychology has moved on quite a bit since then.

Modern personality tests are more accurate and better at predicting what people need to do to succeed. By completing questionnaires and following advice within this book, you'll be guided through seven major dimensions of personality. These have been researched in over half a million people – from groups as varied as chief executives and entrepreneurs to students and soldiers, in countries ranging from the UK and USA to Brazil and China.

Not long ago, the BBC asked me to test the personalities of the celebrities and professional dancers on its hit TV show *Strictly Come Dancing*. My analysis of the celebrities' personality profiles allowed me to make stunningly accurate predictions about how well the couples would get on, how hard they would train and how popular they would be with the general public. The celebrities who shone on the show understood their personalities, their unique strengths.

By understanding your personality and exploring and honing your particular talents, you can chart your very own course to success. Perhaps you work for a large organisation and want to climb the career ladder. Maybe you work for yourself and realise that your livelihood depends on how good you are. Or you may want to be successful in some other endeavour – to be a better parent, a more successful fundraiser, an empire-building entrepreneur. Whatever your goals, you will achieve them by learning more about your personality and following advice that is perfectly designed for you and you alone.

Ready to discover your greatest asset?

01

Making the most of yourself

"Like one's strengths, how one performs is unique. It is a matter of personality."

Peter Drucker, management writer

As a psychologist, I'm fascinated by people and what makes some succeed while others stumble. I've studied many, many high achievers and star performers. I've worked with managing directors, chief executives, salespeople, as well as top sportspeople and a handful of celebrities, such as TV presenters, pop stars, and even a lingerie model. I work with teams and entire organisations to help them to become more effective, more productive, more successful.

What I've noticed is that the smartest, best-educated person doesn't always end up the most successful. Book-smarts only get you so far. I'm sure you can think of people who have brains the size of planets. They're as clever as rocket scientists but have no social skills. On the other hand, you probably know people such as entrepreneurs or businesspeople who didn't go to university or even dropped out of school yet still turned their lives into solid gold successes. They succeeded because of their determination and curiosity, their adaptability and persuasiveness. In other words, they got ahead because of their personal qualities – their personalities.

Personality counts when it comes to getting together too. I work with entire teams to get them working together more effectively. When people in teams understand each other's motivations and ways of thinking, they gel together and work faster; they avoid unnecessary misunderstandings while at the same time igniting constructively creative conflicts. So learn about personality to get a glimpse into how to work more effectively with other people too.

Discover yourself

I've written this book to help you make the most of yourself. Here's how I've structured the book to do exactly that:

- In Chapter 1, I talk you through the concept of 'personality' and how it can help us. I've also included seven questionnaires in this chapter for you to work through. I recommend that you complete all of the questionnaires before moving on; that way you'll get the most from the rest of this book.
- Chapters 2 to 8 cover seven different aspects of personality. Once you've worked through Chapter 1, you should feel free to skip around these chapters. Treat this as your very own pick 'n' mix, choose-your-own-adventure book. If one of the questionnaires in Chapter 1 grabs your attention, go on and jump ahead to that chapter. Questionnaire 1 is explored in Chapter 2, questionnaire 2 in Chapter 3 and so on.
- In Chapter 9, I guide you through a plan of action for bringing everything together and making the most of yourself. Use this chapter to make sure that your good intentions are translated into actions and positive changes that you can incorporate into your work and life.

Let's get started right away with a quick quiz to discover your personality, the stuff that makes you unique. Rather than just *read* about what personality is and how you can make the best of it, how about you pick up a pen and answer a few questions right now?

Questionnaire 1

This is the first of seven short questionnaires. Each one has ten statements. Work through them quickly and tick whether you agree or disagree with each one. To reveal your true personality, work through them as quickly as you can. The longer you mull over each statement, the less accurate your result will be. Tick the answer that's top-of-mind, the one that instinctively feels right.

	Agree	Disagree
1 I usually have several books on the go at the same time.		
2 I often start projects and hobbies that I don't finish.		
3 I can concentrate for long periods of time.		
4 I enjoy puzzles, crosswords and Sudoku.		
5 I rarely visit galleries, museums and exhibitions.		
6 People say that I often come up with great ideas.		
7 I seldom think about philosophical or spiritual questions.		
8 I prefer to make decisions based on facts rather than feelings.		
9 I've always been interested in how things work.		
10 I enjoy reading poetry.		

Make a note of your answers – I'll explain how to score the questionnaire in Chapter 2. Rather than throw lots of questions at you all in one go, I've split them up throughout this chapter. More to come very soon.

What is 'personality' exactly?

Roger Holdsworth, co-founder of consulting firm Saville & Holdsworth and guru of personality measurement, tells me:

‘Personality is the answer to the question: “What is the person like?”’

The way you are is down to your personality, a set of preferences that are written into your brain. To explain properly, let’s go on a quick tour of the brain.

Human beings are the only species to have the ability to engage in conscious thought – to think about the future and make plans, imagine things we’ve never seen and ponder what’s going on in other people’s heads.

But conscious thought requires time and uses energy. Imagine if our prehistoric ancestors had needed to engage in conscious thought for everything. When confronted by a vicious animal, the last thing our early predecessors needed was to contemplate the best course of action. ‘Gosh, that’s an awful lot of teeth on that snarling beast. I wonder why it’s running at me. Hmm, I wonder what should I do?’ Too late – the hungry fiend has already latched its jaws around your leg.

No, our ancestors survived because they developed mental shortcuts that helped them to act swiftly: ‘If I see a scary creature, I run away!’ No question about it, quick as a flash.

Such shortcuts are like your brain’s autopilot – a simple set of rules that your brain follows immediately unless you consciously tell it otherwise. Ancient people may have had simple rules such as ‘If I see food, I stuff it into my mouth and start chewing furiously!’ or ‘If people anger me, I’ll club them over the head.’

We’ve evolved a bit since then. But we still develop new shortcuts to deal with the modern world and avoid the energy-intensive processing of conscious thought. And here’s the important bit: the way these shortcuts are laid down in your brain determines your personality. ‘If X happens, I do Y.’

Your rule might be, 'If I see a stranger, I'll go over and say hello', making you a sociable, gregarious person, for example. Or your rule might be, 'If I see a stranger, I'll drop my gaze and turn away', leading you to come across as more reserved.

I'll talk in more depth about what personality is in a few moments. But it's time for another questionnaire about you.

Questionnaire 2

Here are another ten statements. Again, decide quickly whether you agree or disagree with each one. Avoid spending too long agonising over your answers to get a true reflection of who you are.

	Agree	**Disagree**
1 I rarely feel anxious.		
2 I sometimes get nervous before important events.		
3 Very little in life ever upsets me.		
4 I occasionally have trouble sleeping.		
5 I worry quite a lot.		
6 I'm usually calm in a crisis.		
7 I sometimes feel down without good reason.		
8 I wish that I could worry less.		
9 I'm a relaxed, easy-going person.		
10 I don't let it bother me when people are negative or critical.		

Made a note of your answers? Great, let's move on again.

Is personality nature or nurture?

Are we born with our personalities or do they develop as we grow up?

Bit of both actually.

We're born with some of our personality preferences. Scientists tell us that up to half of our personality may be inherited – down to our genes. In the same way that conditions such as heart disease and high blood pressure are partly hereditary, your personality may be too. Whether you're sociable or reserved, hyper-organised or mega-untidy comes down to sequences of DNA passed on to you from your parents.

However, your genes are only part of the story. They lay down a prototype for your rules, a first draft of the script, and your upbringing refines those initial drafts.

Say you're born with the genes to be sociable and gregarious. If your parents bundle you outside even on cold winter days to play with the other kids on the street, that may reinforce your outgoing nature. But if your parents keep you indoors to study or play computer games on your own, that may revise your script to make you just a little less outgoing.

Or suppose you were brought up by parents who told you off every time your room was untidy. For an easy life, you might react by developing a rule that says, 'If I see a room that's in a mess, I tidy it up.' No need to think about it. Avoid the hassle of being told off by doing it automatically. But if your parents allowed you to leave your room looking like a bomb had hit it, you might grow up with a script that says, 'If I see a room that's in a mess, I know it's no big deal.'

Having these rules or scripts saves time and bother. They tell us how to behave without us having to think too hard.

So how does this help you to succeed?

Once you understand your personality, the rules and scripts that govern your life, you can seek out situations that allow you to play to your strengths. You can find employers and organisations that value you for the way you are. You can seek out friendships and situations that allow you to use your talents. You can compensate for your weaknesses by surrounding yourself with people who are strong where you are weak. Do that and you can succeed. *Really* succeed.

Questionnaire 3

Time for another ten statements. I promise the results will all be revealed soon. For now, just note your immediate reactions to each of the statements.

	Agree	**Disagree**
1 I'm often the centre of attention at social gatherings.		
2 I'm good at telling jokes and making people laugh.		
3 I am a very private person.		
4 I often find myself starting conversations with total strangers.		
5 I select my friends carefully.		
6 I like to have time away from other people to think clearly.		
7 I have lots of friends.		
8 I make new friends quickly and easily.		
9 It takes a long time for other people to get to know me well.		
10 I prefer to listen than talk about myself.		

Rewriting the rules

Not all of our personality scripts are helpful to us as adults. The danger comes when our personalities tell us to behave in ways that stop us from getting the results we want.

So can you change your scripts?

The good news is that you can.

You already do it on a daily basis. Say a friend is wearing an outfit that she adores but you hate. Your gut instinct is 'Ugh!', but when she asks you what you think, you manage to put a smile on your face and say, 'It's lovely!'

Your brain is like a meadow of shoulder-high grass. Every time you make a journey using the same route, you trample down the grass and make the path easier to follow. And by adulthood you have some pretty well-established pathways.

The paths you use the most – perhaps to seek out other people rather than avoid them, or to tidy up your house rather than leave your home in disarray – get stronger and stronger. Your personality reflects the physical reality that some of the connections and routes in your brain are beefier than others.

But you can override your personality. In my career as a coach, I've worked with hundreds of people who have built new habits because they wanted to. And so can you.

Just because a pathway has been trodden down in the tall grass doesn't mean that you can't forge a new one. You can seek a different direction through the meadow, crushing the greenery underfoot to create a new trail. Every time you amble along that new-found pathway, you make it easier the next time. And with continued use, you turn a barely discernible path into a beaten track. You replace your original script with a fresh one, making a new, desirable behaviour second nature.

Questionnaire 4

Pen or pencil at the ready? Remember to work through the statements as quickly as you can.

	Agree	Disagree
1 I enjoy making plans and drawing up lists of things to do.		
2 I usually make up my mind very quickly.		
3 I usually prepare for things well in advance.		
4 I research carefully before making decisions.		
5 I enjoy taking risks.		
6 People would say that I am a spontaneous person.		
7 I aim for perfection in whatever I do.		
8 Planning in advance takes the excitement out of life.		
9 I am careful and pay attention to whatever tasks I do.		
10 I'm often the first to try something new.		

That's four out of the seven quizzes done – more than halfway through now. Only a few to go!

I can't *change* who I am!

A lot of people argue that they can't change the person that they are. Perhaps they tell themselves:

- **'I'm always late.'**

- 'I have a short fuse – I can't help it.'
- 'I'm not very creative – never have been and never will be.'
- 'I'm not very organised – that's just the way I am.'

But people can and do change. Here's a fact for you: anyone can change their behaviour if they make the effort to.

My 60-something-year-old mother always thought that she wasn't very good with technology, but over the last year she has learnt to do loads. She can send emails, shop online and even use a webcam to chat to friends and family all over the world. She learned how to use the timer on her digital camera to take photos of groups so no one has to hold the camera; they can all be in the photo. If my mum can change, you can too.

Never say you can't do something or that you're just built that way. Because those are just excuses that let you off the hook, that allow you to keep repeating unhelpful patterns of behaviour.

Can old dogs really learn new tricks?

Perhaps you're thinking that you're too old to change. Or you've heard the brain only creates a finite number of brain cells and after a certain age, the brain loses hundreds of thousands of brain cells every day, right?

Actually, it's a myth, something that a single piece of research knocks completely on the head. Dr Eleanor Maguire and her team at University College London scanned the brains of taxi drivers and compared them to those of ordinary folk. They found that all of the black cab drivers had a larger hippocampus – the region of the brain that's responsible for navigation. The black-cab drivers who had been driving the longest – some of them for over 40 years – had the largest hippocampus of all.

We now know that the brain produces new neurons throughout our lives – a process known as neurogenesis. Plus the brain continues to build connections between neurons into old age ('neuroplasticity'). It's only a lack of novel experiences and effort that allows your brain to dwindle. In the same way that press-ups build muscles, modern science shows that mental exercises can enlarge areas of the brain. You can grow more brain!

So here's my point. If you want to change, just do it. The next time you hear yourself saying, 'I'm no good at . . .', ask yourself, 'Why the hell not?'

Questionnaire 5

You know the drill by now. Quick as lightning, off you go!

	Agree	Disagree
1 I speak my mind even when people may not enjoy hearing it.		
2 I change my behaviour to fit in with different people.		
3 I am often critical of other people.		
4 I feel upset when I have to turn people down.		
5 I enjoy the cut and thrust of a vigorous debate.		
6 I always make an effort to see the other person's point of view.		
7 I don't care much what other people think of me.		
8 I am usually happy to go along with other people's wishes.		
9 I am not afraid of conflict.		
10 I feel comfortable making a complaint when necessary.		

Small changes for big results

The good news is that many of the changes I suggest in this book are not wholesale modifications to your life but quite small tweaks.

Here's a question for you: how many minutes separate a great surgeon from a lousy one? Yes, you read that right. *Minutes*. Confused? Let me explain.

Researchers in the US looked at the differences between great surgeons and not-so-good ones. There's no National Health Service in the US so patients are free to switch surgeons if they're not happy. So patients rate surgeons all the time, allowing good surgeons to get paid more and bad ones to earn less.

Oddly enough, the researchers were unable to find any differences in surgical skill between top-rated and so-so doctors. The main differences were in how much the surgeons listened, showed compassion and answered questions.

We come back to the question I asked: how many minutes separate a great surgeon from a lousy one? Answer: three minutes. Top-rated surgeons tended to spend, on average, a mere three minutes longer answering questions than their less popular counterparts.

Three minutes of listening. Not a lot is it? But in terms of bringing patients back and how much the doctors earned, it mattered hugely.

Many of the best-kept secrets of success take only minutes each day. I'm not telling you to change the person you are. Only to make minor adjustments, subtle refinements to what you do, to make you more successful.

Questionnaire 6

Here's another ten statements. Work through them quickly.

	Agree	Disagree
1 I read at least a dozen books a year.		
2 I am often the first person to sign up for a new training course.		
3 I believe the best way to learn is by doing rather than reading about it.		
4 People would say that I am an expert in my field.		
5 I read and research thoroughly before any new endeavour.		
6 I hated my days of studying and taking exams.		
7 I would rather read than watch television.		
8 I dislike lectures and seminars.		
9 I know more about my topic than most of the people I know.		
10 I see training courses as an intrusion into my day-to-day job.		

Nearly done – just one more questionnaire to go . . .

If you want it, you can do it

Ever learned a language? I studied a bit of French at school and remember my first faltering steps with the language. I recall going on a week-long camping trip to France and being sent to buy breakfast the first morning. Standing outside the baker's, I literally had to drag from memory the phrase for 'I would like to buy' ('Je voudrais acheter'). Then what's the word for bread? ('pain'). What's the word for 'some'? Do I say, 'du pain' or 'de la pain'? Oh, and of course add in the word 'please'. 'Je voudrais acheter du pain, s'il vous plaît.'

I had to work out what I wanted to say before going in on that first morning, but the next day the conversation got easier and the third day easier still. The more I consciously worked at what I was doing, the more it became second nature.

And you can do the same. The ancient part of your brain – often called the 'lower brain' – is packed with subconscious rules that try to push you to act in immediate, instinctive ways. The lower brain is your autopilot – the mechanism that controls your behaviour when you're not paying attention. You also have a 'higher brain', which is your pilot, the executive control centre. As it happens, this conscious voice in your head allows you to overrule the lower brain when you want to.

Your lower brain may urge you to scream and hit something when you're angry, but your higher brain tells you that punching your boss wouldn't be a good idea. Or your lower brain may tempt you to eat 14 bars of chocolate in one session, but your higher brain decides that it's not the best thing for your waistline.

The more you override your lower brain's scripts and work at changing your behaviour, the more quickly you can adopt a new script. So whatever you want to work on, you only need to *want* to change it and then *practise* it.

Questionnaire 7

And here we have the final ten questions.

	Agree	Disagree
1 I have a clear sense of direction in my life.		✓
2 I would avoid tough challenges and difficult problems if I could.	✓	
3 I have a strong desire to compete and win in everything I do.		✓
4 I enjoy taking charge of other people.		✓
5 I sometimes feel that I'm drifting in life.	✓	
6 I know exactly what I want to get out of my career.		✓
7 I am not a competitive person.	✓	
8 I'm not interested in having authority over others.	✓	
9 I am determined to succeed even if I have to make personal sacrifices.		✓
10 I am a highly ambitious individual.		✓

Usage instructions

Each of the seven questionnaires measures a different dimension of personality. Physical objects can be measured in different ways. There are the standard dimensions of height, length and width. Of course, we can measure how heavy an object is, its weight too. And what about other 'dimensions', such as an object's colour and texture? In the same way that everyday objects, ranging from computers to cardboard boxes, wristwatches to washing machines, can be described in different ways, our personalities can be measured along seven dimensions.

Each of these dimensions is a continuum, a spectrum. For example, you can be extremely outgoing, quite outgoing, a little outgoing or not at all outgoing. You can be super-organised, organised, somewhat disorganised or a complete disaster when it comes to organising. To make the advice in this book work for you, I divide people into high, low or average categories. This is one of the few books you will ever pick up in which you *don't* have to read all of it. You have your own special strong points, but also your own particular challenges, so the advice that will help you to get ahead needs to be tailored to your individual personality profile.

In each chapter, you first add up the points you scored on one of the questionnaires to work out whether you're high, low or average on that dimension. If you're high, you read all of the sections that are meant for high scorers. If you're low, you read only the sections that are meant for low scorers.

But what if you're an average scorer, in the middle? In my experience, most of us need to strive towards the high end of each dimension, so take heed of the advice aimed at low scorers. A few of the pointers aimed at low scorers may not resonate with you, but much of it should still help you to grow, develop and achieve.

Are you starting to wonder what your personality profile looks like yet? We're nearly ready to begin . . .

WARNING! Danger ahead!

Three final questions before we get started. Do you know anyone who's a bit overconfident, sometimes cocky, perhaps even a little arrogant? Probably, I'd guess.

How about someone who's a bit disorganised, quite often turning up late when you're meeting and probably not the most reliable person you know? Certainly, I can think of a few friends like that.

And what about a friend or colleague who's really talkative? The kind who monopolises a conversation and talks about me, me and more me? Yeah, I know that type too.

Of course we all know people like that. There's the danger. We know *other* people who are arrogant, but no, not *us*. We know *other* people who are disorganised, but *you and I* are free spirits, right? We know *other* people who are talkative and poor listeners – *we're* just really entertaining!

How well do we *really* know ourselves?

Do you think that you're a good judge of character? I think *I* am. Do you think that you have a better sense of humour than most people? Sure, I know *I* do. And would you say that you're above average or below average at pleasing your partner in bed? Of course, I know *I'm* above average!

I often speak to groups of several hundred people at a time. I ask people to raise their hands in answer to those three questions. Whether I'm speaking to senior managers or shopfloor workers, self-made businesspeople or MBA students, the answer is usually the same. Pretty much everyone thinks that they are better than most people. Having asked these questions lots and lots of times, I'd say that 90 per cent of people think that they are above average. That doesn't quite add up, does it?

We can all describe the positive aspects of our personalities. But most of us find it easier to spot the negative traits in other people than in ourselves. Our brains look for cunning ways to rationalise and justify our behaviour so we don't feel too down about our real weaknesses. Even a quick flick through TV shows such as *American Idol, The X Factor* and *Britain's Got Talent* illustrate that a *lot* of people don't really understand how they come across.

The questionnaires and advice within this book allow you to diagnose yourself along seven distinct dimensions of personality. Each chapter explains the positive features but also the potential disadvantages of having your particular personality profile. You will probably agree with the positive stuff, but experience tells me that you may bristle at some of the negative stuff.

So before we begin, my advice to you is this: please don't discount immediately what you read. Just because you may not agree with some of the less-than-positive comments doesn't mean that they aren't true about you. If you don't think that's you, ask the opinions of people who know you well and go with what they say.

Time to get on with discovering your personality, your talents, what you're good at. So let's look at the first personality dimension by asking a question: How curious are you?

02

Inquisitiveness

"I know quite certainly that I myself have no special talent; curiosity, obsession and dogged endurance, combined with self-criticism have brought me to my ideas."

Albert Einstein, scientist

If you go to a job interview, you can expect to be asked what you know about the company and why you want to work there. But if you get interviewed by Hugh Bishop, chairman of communications agency Meteorite, you are almost certain to be asked, 'Tell me about your journey to work.'

It's not so much of a question as a request, but let's go with it. So how would *you* reply?

You might say that you usually leave at 7.50 to get the 8.14 train. Perhaps you've figured out the best spot on the platform to wait to get a seat on the train. Maybe you prefer the other end of the platform, to get out of the station as quickly as possible. On the way, you usually grab a tall latté from Starbucks before getting to your desk moments before 9 o'clock.

Or is your journey to work different every day? Sometimes you take the train but occasionally the bus so you can watch the world from a different vantage point. You may leave for work a lot earlier than you need to. That way, you get to explore uncharted parts of town, to discover quirky new cafés, admire the architecture that so many others take for granted or take a stroll through the park on a sunny day.

These two very different approaches to travelling to work illustrate both ends of the Inquisitiveness continuum. People who have High-Inquisitiveness are curious and creative, but perhaps a bit distracted by the next idea, which means that they may not always follow through. People who have Low-Inquisitiveness are pragmatic and good at getting jobs done, but could perhaps be a bit more creative.

Neither one is better than the other. The very best people combine creativity with pragmatism, ideas with follow-through. So how do you stack up on Inquisitiveness?

Your Inquisitiveness

Take a look back at Questionnaire 1 on page 3. Give yourself two points every time you agreed with one of the following statements: 1, 2, 4, 6, 9 and 10. Give yourself two points if you disagreed with each of the statements numbered 3, 5, 7 and 8. You should have a score between 0 and 20.

A score of 10 or less suggests that you are low on Inquisitiveness. A score of 16 or more suggests that you are high on Inquisitiveness. A score of between 12 and 14 suggests that you have average levels of Inquisitiveness.

But don't get too fixated on your precise score. Good psychologists only ever use personality tests to give an *indication* of someone's personality. To find out your true personality, ask the opinions of people who know you well. Read the descriptions of Low- and High-Inquisitiveness people – which do *you* feel the stronger affinity with? Or do you feel you sit between the two?

Remember that in working through the rest of this chapter, you need only read the sections that are aimed at your personality profile. If you're average on Inquisitiveness, read the advice for both ends of the spectrum and pick the advice that seems best suited to you. But bear in mind that the advice within the Low-Inquisitiveness sections may be most useful if you want to boost your creativity.

What kind of person are you?

You can often see differences in Inquisitiveness from an early age. A friend of mine is father to identical twins Alexander and Tobias. Despite being born with the same genetic blueprint, they are already – at the age of ten – exhibiting clear differences in how they behave.

Visiting them one Sunday, I watched Alex spend the afternoon playing with his carpentry set. Toby started drawing a dog they had seen earlier in the park, but then lost interest and ran off to play football before asking if we could play a card game called Yu-Gi-Oh. That game lasted all of 15 minutes before he decided that he was going to make a wooden dog. After a couple of hours, Alex presented me with a charming wooden airplane that he had lovingly sawn and hammered and sanded down. Toby had nothing to show for his efforts, but he'd had fun!

Toby strikes me as being a High-Inquisitiveness child. He has many interests and delights in them all, but has a short attention span and gets distracted easily. Alex strikes me as being a Low-Inquisitiveness child. He has fewer interests, has the ability to concentrate on a task for a long time and enjoys turning his ideas into reality.

A jack of all trades, master of none or jack of few trades, master of one. Which are you?

The science of Inquisitiveness

Some scientists argue that your natural level of Inquisitiveness comes down to how the two halves of your brain, the two hemispheres, work together. The right hemisphere of the brain processes facts and information in a rational, logical fashion; the left hemisphere is more intuitive. So Low-Inquisitiveness people may have right hemispheres that are a bit more dominant. High-Inquisitiveness individuals may have left hemispheres that are more dominant.

The Low-Inquisitiveness person: down-to-earth and reliable

You're a practical, sensible person and often the voice of reason in a group. You prefer to deal with facts and figures than concepts and possibilities. You don't have the time for airy-fairy ideas. You want to have answers rather than debate questions.

In fact, you probably get a bit frustrated by people who have their heads up in the clouds. They talk about amazing ideas, but you know from experience that their words rarely get turned into actions. You want to understand how an idea will help you to do your job better right now. If it doesn't translate into a tool, a product, a service that you can use now or soon, you'd rather not waste too much time thinking about it.

You don't set out to destroy others' ideas, but you do want to know how they will help you. What are the benefits? How is it useful? What does it mean in practical terms?

You prefer to get on with a task rather than ponder or debate endlessly the best way of doing it. In fact, you have a phenomenal gift for getting things done. While some others are still debating concepts and ideas, you've rolled your sleeves up and are getting on with it. You don't get distracted by 'What if . . . ?' questions. If there's a problem, you look to see what's worked in the past. You draw on past experience and tried-and-tested solutions. If it worked on a previous occasion, it may work this time too. Why reinvent the wheel?

The High-Inquisitiveness person: blue skies and outside the box

If there was such a job as the CCO (Chief Creativity Officer), that'd be you.

You're a curious, imaginative, ingenious, big-picture person who yearns to understand how everything works. Some people say that curiosity killed the cat, but you'd rather be dead than stop asking questions. You enjoy soaking up new ideas and you're probably the kind of person who loves to dream, to ask, 'What if . . . ?' You find it maddening when people ask a question and want only a single answer. You delight in thinking about what *could* be rather than being bound by what is or what happened in the past.

You have a formidable knack for taking ideas from different worlds and bringing them together in interesting and enlightening ways. You can connect concepts that others may see as unrelated and see patterns where others see only confusion. You can always be depended on to bring fresh perspectives to a discussion. To devise original solutions to old problems and come up with new, sometimes smoking-hot, ideas. Some of your colleagues or the people around you may sometimes think your ideas a bit wild and crazy, but that's because they don't have your imagination.

You know that you have a short attention span. You get bored easily and you'd hate to do just one thing for the rest of your life. You have so many interests – among them you're probably a fan of classical music, opera, poetry and art. You feel that there is so much deliciousness in the world for you to do and experience. If only there were enough time to do it all!

Make the most of yourself – for Low-Inquisitiveness people

You thrive in work and life when you spend most of your time on practical matters rather than abstract ideas and fanciful possibilities. So learn that you will succeed and feel most fulfilled when you find that sweet spot.

Make good choices in your work and life. Don't try to compete with those pretentious types with their heads in the clouds. I will tell you in the rest of this section that creativity has value – a lot of value sometimes. But working with concepts, theories and new ideas should be the extra little something that helps you to be more successful, rather than the way you spend the bulk of your time.

Ensure you can spend a significant chunk of your time as a doer, in being hands-on and applying the skills you have. Do that and you'll be not only satisfied but productive too.

Be ready to think outside the box

"The key to success is to risk thinking unconventional thoughts. Convention is the enemy of progress."

Trevor Bayliss, inventor

I used to work with someone, a fellow psychologist, who was extremely high on Inquisitiveness. Sebastian was the go-to guy if you were wrestling with a problem and needed creative inspiration. His ideas were often a little too quirky or entirely out of this world, but no one could doubt his inventiveness.

One day he announced that he was quitting. His decision sent shock waves around the company because he had been both popular and good at his job. He was going to set up a company to offer psychology-based coaching over the Internet. We thought he'd finally lost his marbles. Psychology via a computer screen? How on earth would that work? Even as the bosses waved him goodbye, they privately muttered that it would never work. His venture would be a flop, he'd be begging for his job back.

But his company, The Mind Gym, took off and is an enormous hit. A transatlantic success story with hundreds of employees that has trained tens of thousands of people.

Being down-to-earth and practical may get you through a lot of situations in life. If there's a problem, you probably know the right way to deal with it. Doing the same as you've always done may not be enough though – you could get caught in a deep mental rut. Sometimes you need a novel approach to give you that competitive edge. Yes, we're talking about ways to see the world through fresh perspectives, applying your knowledge in original ways and becoming more creative, innovative, even occasionally revolutionary. Want to know how?

Can we *really* become more creative?

Creativity isn't something that you're either born with or without. We all begin life with the capacity to explore, play, wonder how the world worked and create. Growing up, you may have stifled that part of yourself, labelling it childish. But becoming creative is a skill you can revive.

The human brain is naturally lazy – it craves the easiest path, not the most creative one. When you come across a problem, your brain tries to save energy by looking in its databank for a solution that has worked before, by recycling. Why waste energy coming up with a novel solution when an old one will do?

But you can force your brain to be more creative with conscious effort. If you pose bigger or different questions than it's used to answering, you can tempt your sluggish brain to switch into a higher gear and come up with something new.

Stuff more into your brain

> "Creativity is the power to connect the seemingly unconnected."
>
> **William Plomer, novelist**

Ever wondered what would happen if you threw a shoe or an iPod into a blender? No? The website www.willitblend.com has videos showing a household blender chopping and shredding everything from a Rubik's cube to a cola can. Some people ask, 'Why on earth would they want to do that?' But *why not*?

People who are naturally high on Inquisitiveness ask, 'Why not?' They constantly explore the world, poke their noses into anything and everything, and process it all with a sense of wonderment.

Breakthrough ideas are often merely old ideas put together in different ways – happy accidents. They often turn out to be existing thoughts and concepts but assembled from seemingly unconnected spheres, crunched together in an as yet unseen fashion or taken to illogical but creative conclusions. And you can learn to do this too.

In the same way that lifting weights can turn scrawny biceps into bulging ones, you can beef up your creativity. You can establish new pathways in your brain that allow you to make fresh associations and see new patterns in the world.

Become your best: Gathering experiences

Get yourself a:

- digital camera or camera phone
- notebook (and pen)
- folder, box, scrapbook or bulletin board.

Use the camera to capture images of gorgeous architecture, graphics, clothing – anything and everything that piques your interest. Use the notebook to scribble thoughts, observations, feelings. Find a camera and notebook that are both small enough for you to carry with you most of the time. No point having them if they end up being left at home! Fill the folder or bulletin board with newspaper cuttings, pages from brochures, ticket stubs, swatches of fabric and anything else that catches your attention. Fashion designers and advertising creatives often jam images and textures together to create mood boards and collages.

But what should you *do* with these photos, notes and bits and pieces? Actually, what you do with them is less important than the fact that you're noticing them, collecting them and shoving the information deep into the recesses of your brain. Because this is about retraining your awareness and how you see the world.

Highly creative people live in the same world as everyone else – they just pay attention to it differently. So taking snaps and collecting scraps of paper and snippets of junk is about getting you used to seeing the world with Inquisitiveness-coloured spectacles.

Everything you photograph, cut out or save is expanding the way you look at the world. Whether someone else judges your items 'useful' or not is irrelevant. If *you* think they're interesting, that's all the reason you need to keep them.

'Anything can be an inspiration. I take photographs and notes of everything around me, such as the logos and stickers I see on vans, exhibitions of flower displays and mixed fabric collages and modern art sculptures created by local college students,' says Emma Leah Jones, owner of virtual assistant and business support company My Little Angel.

Speaking personally, I keep track of words and phrases that I like. Some of them currently include: alchemy, harrowing, forgo, impasse, rife, ruckus and death-defying. I don't know how I might use them, but logging experiences and words helps my brain to register them and maybe exploit them at a later date. And you can do the same for your brain with words, images, smells or textures that you come across.

Composer John Cage once said, 'I think people who are not artists often think artists are inspired. But if you work at your art, you don't have time to be inspired. Out of the work comes the work.' So there you go. Creativity doesn't come from mere inspiration – it comes from putting in the work.

Enhance your creativity one step at a time

A client in the advertising industry once said to me, 'Doing things the same way sacrifices future possibilities, the chance that something could be better or even wonderful.'

I don't know about you, but I'm certainly guilty of getting stuck in the same old routine. From how I get ready for work and the journey I take to the office, to the way I exercise at the gym and my favourite restaurants for dinner. I have routines that mean I don't need to think too hard. I can coast on autopilot. This is, of course, terrible for creativity. No new stimuli means no new thoughts!

One of the best ways to enhance your creativity is to try fresh ideas and experiences. In fact, just try out one idea a week. It doesn't have to be anything earth-shattering to begin with. I'm not suggesting you move out of your home and live in a grass hut. Merely change one of your daily rituals and routines.

Perhaps buy a different newspaper for a week. Have an apple instead of a biscuit with your mid-morning coffee. Listen to classical music if you're more into chart hits. Get up an hour earlier or take a different route to work for a week.

Start with small changes and move on to larger ones. Mix things up and see how even small alterations can affect how you see the world.

One idea a week makes for 52 ideas in a year. You can do that, can't you?

Over to you

There's no time like the present. Write down three ways in which you could adjust your daily patterns:

- ....
- ....
- ....

Consider those three your starting point. Remember that you should be aiming for many, many more changes over the coming weeks and months.

Move on to bigger leaps of creativity too

Making small changes in your life should only be a start. How about exploring a handful of occasional, bigger ventures too? Artists and designers don't sit in a room waiting for inspiration to strike. High-Inquisitiveness people throw themselves into new experiences, tastes, settings and situations to fuel their imagination. It's the difference between reading about dolphins and swimming with them, splashing around with and experiencing it up close.

Perhaps take a drive to visit a country pub you've never been to. Go to an exhibition or gallery even though you know it's not your usual thing and try to imagine what the artist felt. Visit a toy shop and pick up a handful of toys, asking yourself what's distinctive about them – their texture, the technical features, the emotional associations. Or ask a friend to introduce you to a hobby or sport you've never tried – it could be anything from online computer gaming to horse riding. Doesn't matter what it is, so long as you're expanding your awareness of what else is out there.

Over to you

Can you commit to a handful of bigger experiences over the next few months? Write down three ways in which you will expose yourself to different situations and challenge yourself:

- ....
- ....
- ....

Consume and collect experiences, not things. Mihaly Csikszentmihalyi, psychology professor at Claremont Graduate University in California, has found from his research that 'creativity generally involves crossing the boundaries of domains'.

By adjusting your daily patterns, you help your brain to cross those boundaries and make new associations. You never know when a great idea may pop into your head. But the more you experience and experiment, the more likely it is that you'll get that creative flash.

Soon you may find yourself using ideas from the domains of agriculture, music or anthropology to further your productivity at work. Or you might use psychology, art or animal husbandry to become a better parent. And so it goes on.

The key is to mix it up. Keep experimenting and see what works.

Create bigger problems for yourself

Here's an idea a client shared with me: 'Whenever my team is facing a problem, I always say, "That's not a big enough problem. How can we make this problem bigger?"'

I liked his idea and I've used it a lot since then.

Suppose an engineer poses the question, 'How can we make the internal combustion engine more efficient?' That focuses the other engineers on incremental improvements – tweaks – that may eke out an additional few percentage points of efficiency.

Or we could make the problem bigger and ask, 'How can we get a family from A to B for the lowest cost possible?' That gives the members of the team wider scope to deploy their creativity. They could consider ideas such as building electric cars, solar-powered cars, cars with mini fusion reactors, cars that run on tramlines or float like plastic pods on monorails, even sleds, bikes, helicopters and flying machines.

Sure, some of the ideas might be crazy, but some might be precisely what you need. After all, when Henry Ford built the first mass-produced car, most people at the time thought he was crazy. They sneered and said, 'The car will never replace the horse-drawn cart!'

History is filled with examples of people who asked bigger, different questions.

Back in the golden age of radio, engineers asked the question, 'How can we reduce interference so that listeners can hear crisper, clearer music and speech?' One engineer took an idea to his bosses for a radio that also included pictures. They dismissed the idea, arguing that it wasn't what they were looking for. So he took it to their competitor RCA, and they built the first working prototype of a television set. Rather than asking, 'How can we better entertain people using the radio?' he asked, 'How can we better entertain people?'

Supermarket giant Tesco didn't settle by asking, 'How can we sell more groceries?' It asked, 'How can we make more money?' Now it sells everything from mobile phones and flat-screen TVs to children's shoes and pet insurance.

So rather than asking, 'How can we make our product sell better?' ask, 'What can we make that would sell better?' Don't ask, 'How can I write this report more quickly?' ask, 'How can I get out of writing this report?' Same goes for 'How can I get my boss to give me more interesting projects?' – ask instead, 'What kind of interesting projects do I want – whether they're at this company or not?'

Big problems may not always lead to big breakthroughs. But I'm willing to bet that little problems never do. Before you invest your energies in finding the right solution to a quandary, give a little thought instead to how you can make the whole situation go away.

Aim for quantity of ideas and you'll get quality too

When we consider ways to solve a problem, the first idea we come up with is rarely the most creative. We're not going to win awards for it. The late Linus Pauling, who *did* win awards (a

Nobel Prize for chemistry *and* the Nobel Peace Prize), argued that science is about coming up with *lots* of ideas and then discarding the ineffective ones.

Quality and quantity are not mutually exclusive. By coming up with a greater number of ideas, you may often surprise yourself with their quality too. When was the last time you considered 20 different ways to tackle a problem?

Yes, I'm talking about brainstorming.

OK, I admit it. Brainstorming gets a bad rep. Low-Inquisitiveness people often hate it, rolling their eyes at the mere thought of having 'yet another brainstorm'. You may feel that you could be *doing* things rather than tossing ideas around. The problem is that people often end up restricting themselves to ideas that seem 'sensible', basing their ideas on what worked in the past.

There's a famous saying: 'If you always do what you've done before, don't be surprised when you get the same result.' If every idea has to be both sensible and have worked in the past, how will we ever come up with new products or original inventions?

Whether you're brainstorming with a group or brainstorming on your own, it works. I know it's an established technique and you already know the basic rules, but I'll give you a few twists on the classic method to make sure you get more out of your brainstorming sessions.

Over to you

We all know the rules of brainstorming, right? To check that you do, here's a checklist of six points. Only five of them are true. Can you spot the one I made up?

1 Generate as many ideas as possible. The focus should initially be on *quantity* rather than quality.

2 Suspend judgement. Accept that no idea is a 'bad' idea – no one should be allowed to criticise an idea until after all the ideas have been generated.

3 Write down every idea, no matter how sensible or silly, outlandish or obvious.

4 Combine and improve. Look for ways to build on, expand on, or exaggerate earlier ideas in ever more offbeat ways.

5 Brainstorm before lunch rather than after lunch. Hungry people think better.

6 Review and evaluate ideas only *after* the group has finished brainstorming.

Number 5 is the fib. Kind of obvious, wasn't it?

OK, you do know how to make brainstorming work, but the people around you probably break the rules without realising. Make sure to remind them of the rules of the game.

Become your best: Brainstorming 2.0

Research shows that *traditional* brainstorming doesn't actually work very well. So here are three ways to get more out of it:

- **Ban praise.** Perhaps the biggest danger in brainstorming is that people tend to judge. Some ideas get rewarded with comments such as 'Great idea!' Others get punished with the absence of eye contact and a stony silence – the rest of the group may as well get daggers out and stab the poor idea to death. So here's the key: just as no one should put down a bad idea, people should be banned from praising ideas too.

- **Work individually first.** Groups tend to be heavily influenced by the most senior individuals in the room. So when the boss goes in one direction, perhaps saying, 'We need to do something in the Far East', the group tends to follow suit. The solution: kick off the creative process by asking people to brainstorm individually first. Give every person in the room a pack of Post-it notes. Tell them to spend five or even ten minutes writing down as many ideas on their own as possible. Then put them in a big pile, swirling them together so that the ideas are more anonymous and people feel less openly judged. The aim isn't to discuss who suggested what, but to use those initial ideas as a jumping-off point for further group brainstorming. I know it may feel strange to have a group of people sat brainstorming individually in silence. But research shows that an initial bout of individual brainstorming increases both the quantity *and* quality of creative ideas. Make no mistake, this individual brainstorming thing shouldn't be an option – it's *essential* for effective brainstorming.
- **Set a numerical target.** The third major pitfall is settling for a suggestion too early. Researchers tell us that the most effective brainstorming sessions run for *at least* 40 ideas. You may often be able to combine your later, wild ideas with early, more practical ones to craft quite breathtaking solutions to the problems and challenges you face. I ran a brainstorming session at a credit card company recently and their favourite idea to take forward was actually the seventy-third one!

Kids get it right. They're not afraid to ask so-called 'stupid' questions because they think the answers are obvious. A big part of brainstorming effectively and becoming more creative is learning to interrogate the world with the innocence and naivety of a child again.

So get used to brainstorming, freewheeling, throwing around crazy ideas and seeing who can come up with the wildest ones.

Only when you have a big fat pile of far-out ideas should you review them, see how they might work and choose a handful to take forward.

Take brainstorming to the nth level

Brainstorming has been around for decades. But that's good news as a lot of very smart psychologists, economists and business school professors have studied the technique to see how to get great results. Here are three easy-to-use ideas to throw into the mix, either singly or perhaps together.

Introduce constraints

You'd think that having rules or constraints would *reduce* creativity, but that's not how our brains work. Our poor brains can't cope with too much information. There are literally an infinite number of ideas out there and, when there are no limits, our brains can't decide what to focus on. So they shut down, becoming less creative. Use the following examples to inspire your own brainstorming constraints:

- 'Only products that we can sell for less than £200.'
- 'Only services that we can aim at women.'
- 'Only products that we can sell online.'
- 'Only improvements that we can make by the end of the week.'
- 'Only ideas that our grandparents would understand.'

Introduce time pressure

Do you work better when you know there's no deadline or when the pressure's on? Most people get that little bit more fired up when there's an element of time pressure. And they're no different when it comes to brainstorming.

Avoid saying, 'We can spend as much time on this as we need.' Instead, give people a cut-off: 'We've only got 15 minutes to brainstorm. Once our time's up, we'll choose our top three ideas. The clock's ticking – let's start!'

Make it a contest

Do you like to win? Even if *you* don't, I'll bet you know someone who does. So introduce an element of competition into your brainstorming.

Split your group into smaller groups of perhaps two or three people. Tell them that the winner will be the group that comes up with the greatest *number* of ideas. Offer a small prize or just make it a competition for competition's sake. Then set a time limit and watch the creative sparks fly.

Make the most of yourself – for High-Inquisitiveness people

You feel most alive when you get to be creative. So you will succeed when you recognise this gift and play to your strengths. Make sure that your work and life allow you plenty of opportunities to consider possibilities and throw around ideas.

Perhaps your current situation isn't giving you enough space to create at the moment, but look to the future. Steer clear of jobs and circumstances that require you to get mired in detail and routine – no matter how well intentioned or well paid such opportunities might be. Remember, when you're considering a change in your life, a new job, settling down with a new partner, a fresh project, whatever, that you get bored easily. Ask yourself, 'Will this situation allow me to create, inspire, wonder and be myself most – or at least *some* – of the time?'

Consider the flip-side of creativity

Let's face it. Some of your ideas are kissed by genius – they're that good. But that strength comes with an attendant weakness.

A friend of mine, Christina, exemplifies High-Inquisitiveness. She'll send an email to a dozen friends saying that she's found a stunning new restaurant and she'd like to get us all together for dinner, but she never follows up. She once sent me an email asking for my waist size. I'm sure she'd had some flash of inspiration, but I never found out what it was. Having read about Dubai in the Middle East and how you can camp in the desert under the stars, she suggested that a group of us go there to bring in the New Year. Yes, you guessed it, it never happened. And it drives most of us, her friends, crazy!

The same goes for the world of work too. Micael Dahlén, professor of business administration and marketing strategy at the Stockholm School of Economics, defines business creativity as 'the *concrete* development of products'. I added the emphasis to the word 'concrete'. No point having great ideas unless they get turned into reality. Unless they result in actual products or services, tools or improvements to the way you work and live.

You're a dreamer, a visionary, a powerhouse of creativity. But consider the flip-side. If you spend too much of your time in the world of ideas, you risk becoming someone who 'talks a good game', but never delivers. So here are a handful of ways to make sure that you can have your head in the clouds *and* your feet firmly on the ground.

Learn to recycle

> "We must beware of needless innovation."
>
> **Sir Winston Churchill, prime minister**

Let's go back 50 years. To the early days of the space race when both the Americans and Russians were trying to be the first to get into space and then to the moon. Apparently, both sides spent a lot of time wondering what the most suitable writing instrument would be to take into orbit. NASA spent millions of dollars crafting a 'space pen'. The Russians just packed pencils.

OK, that may be an urban myth, but you get the point. Why reinvent the wheel when it gets the job done? Sometimes 'good enough' will do. You don't need to aim for astonishing solutions to mundane problems.

Take software programmers. A friend tells me that computer programmers often have to decide whether to reuse code from a previous project or craft something new. Novice programmers often start from scratch every time, which works for small projects. But experienced programmers learn to build on the efforts of others rather than reinventing everything all over again. The final solution may not be as elegant, but a software team can get there more quickly and for less cost than if they'd done it *all* themselves.

The same may be true of business in general. I was recently on a BBC TV programme with Theo Paphitis, a 'dragon' from the popular *Dragons' Den* show. He said, 'I've never had an original idea in my life.' He argued that you don't necessarily need to do anything different from your competitors; you only need to do it better. He emphasised that executing what you know may often deliver better results than chasing the next idea. It's worked for him – he's the multimillionaire chairman of stationery chain Ryman and owns stakes in lingerie chain La Senza and gift company Red Letter Days.

The lesson is this: consider the perpetual trade-off between creativity and economy. Developing something new and amazing doesn't happen overnight. Sometimes merely tweaking what you've already got may be good enough. Don't fall into the trap of being constantly creative for creativity's sake.

Become your best: Keeping your Inquisitiveness in check

We are increasingly encouraged to reuse or recycle plastic carrier bags rather than waste resources. 'Do you need a bag for that?' asks the cashier when I buy a solitary pint of milk. In the same way, think, 'Do I really need a new idea for that?' Might you be better off working with what you've already got?

Take people with you

"Don't worry about people stealing your ideas. If your ideas are any good, you'll have to ram them down people's throats."

Howard Aiken, computer pioneer

Having a brain that's like a hothouse of creativity, you see possibilities and futures that others may consider too far-flung. You jump from A to Z with no steps in between. Problem is, the people around you may not be so quick to follow.

An executive I coached once said, 'I do the dreamy stuff. If others can't pick it up and make it happen, that's not my problem, is it?'

'Actually,' I told him, 'it *is* your problem.' A great idea isn't much use if people don't adopt it. The best idea in the world can get left behind, forgotten, if people don't understand how to use it and why they should use it. And if that happens, you may as well never have had the brainchild in the first place. When selling your ideas, your main challenge is helping your less inquisitive buddies and colleagues to relate to your high concepts.

Become your best: Working out the answer to 'So what?'

People are less interested in *what* your idea is than *why* they should use it.

So work out the benefits of your idea. An ex-manager of mine always asked, 'So what?' Whenever I took proposals to him, he always asked this same question – and it's a good one.

Focus on explaining the benefits rather than the features. That a camera has the latest RS954 DigiSync processor isn't going to make most people sit up and take notice. Telling them that they can take idiot-proof, blur-free photos might. That a pane of glass has a hydrophobic aluminium dioxide coating isn't going to have homeowners jumping up and down. But telling them that they never need clean their windows just might. So before you try to convince everyone that your idea is worthwhile, ask yourself:

- Who does it help? An individual, their organisation, family, community?
- What's the point? What difference does it make?

Next, work out your headline statement. Think of a simple, snappy way to summarise your idea. Be ruthless and pare it down to its core – in the same way that journalists use headlines to draw your attention to a newspaper article. Even if it's a massive oversimplification, the point is to give non-believers a way to get the gist of your idea and not get confused by detail, the science, jargon.

When movie producers wanted the go-ahead to make the Sigourney Weaver sci-fi classic *Alien*, they pitched it to studio executives as '*Jaws* in space.' When I run day-long competency-based interviewing training courses, I describe it as 'Helping managers to hire the right people by weeding out liars and exaggerators.' A friend spent three years on a research project entitled 'Impact of education and peer support systems on intention to exercise and exercise adherence'. But what did it mean?

When he was looking for funding, he summed it up as 'How to make fat people thin'.

Oversimplifications, sure. But better for people to get the general idea than no idea at all.

You need persistence to get new ideas to stick, because you're fighting people's natural inertia. Most people find it easier to make do with what they already know, how they've always been doing things, than to do something different. Simply stating an idea once won't be enough to get everyone rushing around in anticipation of how it could transform their lives.

Become your best: Looking to the past to change the future

High-Inquisitiveness individuals naturally explore possibilities and look towards the future. But what already exists or existed in the past may give you a valuable steer on how your new idea may go down. So do your research. Consider the precedents for your proposal:

- What happened when you (or anyone else) tried to introduce similar concepts? Whether you're suggesting a groundbreaking idea or a small tweak, how were other comparable ideas received?
- Why did those previous ideas fail or succeed? What – or who – were the biggest barriers?
- What can you learn from this in applying your current idea? How can you pitch or present your idea to give it the best shot at succeeding?

If you want an idea to flourish, you have to share it. Get people involved so that they aren't just knowledgeable about the workings of your idea but fired up about it too. Convert them into supporters to back you up in meetings, advocates who will speak up for your ideas when you're not there and sponsors to throw their time and resources behind you.

And that's only the beginning. People fall back into old habits so easily. So you need to hold their hands, answer their questions, keep reminding them of the benefits. Then remind them some more.

Become your best: Turning an idea into reality

Chances are you find yourself surrounded by people who are considerably less Inquisitive than you. Most people *claim* that they're open-minded to fresh ideas, but you know better. So think about the best way to get your ideas across, build support for them and win people over. Here's a three-step guide:

1 **Talk it through.** Whether it's an idea at work or something for your home, always get a second opinion. Before you pitch your idea to everyone, do a run-through with someone you trust. That way, you can make sure that your idea makes sense. If the logic ain't clear and compelling to your confidant, it won't be clear to your wider audience.

2 **Identify your key stakeholders.** You can then figure out the best way to get them on your side. If you're trying to launch a new product at work, you may need to coax your boss to let you spend time developing it, the finance director to put up the money, the marketing team to pull together a brochure and so on. If you're trying to convince your kids to eat more broccoli, then your kids are one group of stakeholders, but, if you're clever, you might persuade their cool friend from school – the kid they look up to – to eat broccoli when you invite him over for dinner one night too.

3 **Convince your stakeholders.** People are seldom convinced by facts and figures alone. Think about all the various ways that you can persuade people to listen to you. It may be a clear business case,

financial incentives or inspirational stories that lift them. Other times, you may need to trade favours, call in debts or even use flattery or emotional blackmail!

And don't underestimate how much patience you will need, how much detail you may need to go into. I'll give you an example. Most people know that they should do more exercise and eat healthily, right? But those same people don't do these things because they're used to the path of least resistance – sitting on the sofa and eating ready meals. They need to be shown what kinds of exercises they should be doing, how often and how strenuous. They need to be told how to read food labels and cook food that's healthy and the kids will enjoy. And then they need to be encouraged, gently prodded, nudged and reminded some more.

Ideas don't speak for themselves. *You* have to speak up for your ideas, market them, even hype them a little. Having an idea is only the start of the journey; make sure that you can complete the trip by turning your idea into something that people can use.

Partner up

Grrr! Do Low-Inquisitiveness people frustrate you? They're so cautious of breakthrough ideas, experiences and ways of working. They want to do things as they've always been done. Even when you present them with fresh ideas, they get snarled up in the details rather than seeing the bigger picture. Truth is, you probably think of them as uninspired, dull, lacking in imagination.

All the same, they can be the perfect people to offset your mentally agile nature.

This was the challenge when I worked one-on-one with Paul, a media executive. Paul was responsible for creating new concepts and formats for television programmes. Everyone recognised that he had great ideas, but he had a patchy track record when it came to pitching ideas to TV channels. This meant that few of his programmes were ever made. He was told that his ideas weren't thought through properly. That he didn't think about how much it would cost, how long it would take, who needed to be involved, how it would happen.

So he simply decided to stop pitching ideas. He gave that responsibility to one of his colleagues, Annette, who wasn't known for her creativity. But she could ask Paul the difficult questions, forcing him to articulate more clearly what was only half-formed in his head. She could put budgets together, work out shooting schedules, give clear and concise presentations to TV chiefs, and coordinate the rest of the activities that Paul couldn't. A match made in heaven.

Perhaps opposites *do* attract – or at least can complement each other's preferences and skills.

Who would your perfect partner be?

ONWARDS AND UPWARDS

Remember that the personality dimension Inquisitiveness is a continuum. Neither end of the spectrum is innately more desirable than the other. People who may be too high on it may be creative yet a little detached from reality. People who are too low may be grounded but sometimes lacking in imagination. The ideal is to bridge the divide between the creativity of High-Inquisitiveness and the pragmatism of Low-Inquisitiveness – between imagining and doing.

Here's a quick summary of words and phrases that broadly distinguish Low-Inquisitiveness from High-Inquisitiveness. As you can see, both profiles have strengths and shortcomings.

Low-Inquisitiveness	High-Inquisitiveness
Enjoy being pragmatic doers.	Enjoy being visionary dreamers.
Ask, 'How is this going to work?'	Ask, 'What if . . . . ?'
Tend to be detail-orientated	Focus on the big picture.
Have fewer interests but greater depth.	Have many interests but little depth.
May be perceived as lacking imagination.	May be perceived as lacking follow-through.
Best at execution – turning ideas into reality.	Best at exploration – coming up with ideas.

If you scored lower on Inquisitiveness:

- Appreciate that what has worked in the past may not always be good enough in the future. Hard work isn't enough on its own to get ahead. In a rapidly changing world, you need both good ideas *and* hard work.
- Remember, creativity is a habit that can be nurtured. Make time in your schedule to explore the world and expose yourself to fresh experiences, capturing and documenting them as you go to encourage your brain to absorb them.
- Introduce occasional brainstorming sessions or set your sights on solving bigger problems than the one you appear to be faced with. Many breakthroughs come from looking at the bigger picture or considering notions that at first seem outrageous.

If you scored higher on Inquisitiveness:

- Remember, no one has reinvented the wheel for good reason. Fight your natural urge to recreate *everything*. Ask yourself, 'Is there anything that I can use or adapt rather than create something from scratch?'

- Recognise that innovation requires equal parts of exploration (coming up with ideas) and exploitation (turning ideas into reality). You're hot on exploration; not so hot on exploitation. Be sure to share your ideas, repeat the message and be patient in ensuring that they are adopted. Ideas that aren't used may as well not exist.
- Find people around you who are formidable on implementation. Play to each other's strong points – you focus on the visionary stuff; allow others to make it happen.

03

Resilience

"I have not failed. I've just found 10,000 ways that won't work."

Thomas Edison, inventor

When I met Richard Parks on my first day at university as a bright-eyed 18-year-old, I couldn't have predicted that he would remain one of my closest friends today – nearly 20 years on. But I would *never* have believed anyone if they had predicted that he would also become one of my most successful friends. He laughed all the time and, to be honest, I thought he was kind of goofy at first. So how did he become one of the *richest* people I know?

Richard is currently an executive vice-president of a software business. Five years ago, he and his former business partners sold a previous business, netting him a pay-off in the mid seven figures. But what makes him a marvel is the adversity he has overcome through the years.

Having completed a degree and PhD in physics, he tried to find work as a university lecturer. He applied for over 200 jobs all over the world, but was knocked back every single time. To pay the bills he took menial jobs, working in a kitchen and then a newsagent. Only after 18 months did he give up hope of working at a university to take a job as a financial analyst for an investment bank.

When he and his wife were expecting their first child, the doctors diagnosed their daughter with a rare heart defect that needed extensive surgery at a specialist hospital 80 miles away. Richard and his wife sold their lovely house and rented a small flat to be near their daughter for the year and four touch-and-go operations to give their infant daughter the chance of a full life. It was during this gruelling life-and-death period that a down-turn in banking led to him being made redundant.

Despite all of these setbacks, Richard has never been anything less than composed and resolute. He has always managed to get on with his lot in life. He has coped with rejection, his daughter's ill health, redundancy, as well as the other day-to-day setbacks that we all experience.

How do some people suffer anything from minor hiccups to severe setbacks and manage to carry on? We can all think of people who never really got over a relationship break-up or those who still harbour bitterness over not getting a promotion or losing their job – even years down the line. No one could have blamed Richard if he had broken down, but he didn't. Because he possesses the gift of resilience, which is both a personality trait *and* a quality that you can cultivate.

Your Resilience

Head back to Questionnaire 2 on page 6. Give yourself two points every time you agreed with one of the following statements: 1, 3, 6, 9 and 10. Give yourself two points if you disagreed with each of the statements 2, 4, 5, 7 and 8. You should have a score between 0 and 20.

A score of 8 or less suggests that you're a Low-Resilience individual. A score of 14 or more suggests that you are a High-Resilience person. A score of between 10 and 12 suggests that you have average levels of Resilience.

Read through the rest of this chapter and pick out the sections that are aimed at your personality profile. Remember that your score is only a rough indicator of your true personality. Which end of the spectrum do *you* identify most strongly with? If you're average on Resilience, you will probably benefit more from the advice aimed at Low-Resilience scorers – most of us could do with being more (rather than less) confident in the face of adversity.

What kind of person are you?

If you're sensible, you may have a smoke alarm in your home. Some smoke alarms are incredibly sensitive, going off at the merest whiff of lightly burnt toast. But I remember living in an old house where the kitchen smoke alarm hardly ever went off.

A friend once set a pan of pork chops on fire. Flames shot out of it, sending smoke billowing across the room, and still the smoke alarm didn't make a peep.

Your level of Resilience is determined by your brain's smoke alarm – its early warning system. A small almond-shaped structure in your lower brain called the amygdala looks out for potential threats. Once your amygdala spots a hazard, it sends adrenaline coursing through your veins, makes your heart beat faster and makes you feel tense, wary and prepped for fight or flight. This was all very useful to our ancestors – those primitive humans for whom even a rustle in a bush could have meant being eaten by a ravenous animal.

Low-Resilience people have alarm systems that go off a little too often; High-Resilience people have alarms that perhaps don't go off quite as much as they should. Irrespective of how your system is wired, you can learn how to make better use of it.

The Low-Resilience person: your own worst enemy

You want to do a good job, be liked and be successful. But you worry about what could go wrong and you agonise over the mistakes of the past.

You know that your tendency to worry gets worse when the pressure's on – perhaps when there's a deadline or someone watching over your shoulder. Or if it's a bigger challenge than you're used to dealing with. You can't help thoughts popping into your head, saying:

- 'This is all going to go horribly wrong.'
- 'Oh no, I shouldn't have done that!'
- 'I can't do this – it's too difficult.'

Your worrying can be a good thing though. You're very aware of your shortcomings and you try to fix them. When people point out that you've done something wrong, you remember it. You make a mental note and try ever so hard not to mess up again.

Add to that your aptitude for spotting potential problems in projects and tasks. Other people may look at the future with rose-tinted spectacles, but you have a critical eye and can put bad ideas and initiatives out of their misery straight away.

You wish you could fret less, but you can't seem to help it. In a way, you are your own worst enemy. You're much more critical of yourself than other people are of you. You're much more concerned about your work, your home and the state of the world than most other people. Looking back, you realise that you probably worried about some things that actually didn't turn out so badly in the end. Wouldn't it be great if you could worry a bit less and keep those roiling emotions under control? And learn to bounce back just that little bit more quickly?

The High-Resilience person: serenity personified

You're the kind of person who is calm, composed and cool-headed. It takes a lot to faze you. Even when a customer is shouting and screaming at you about her missing shipment, or when your boss tells you that he's got to make you redundant, you remain unruffled. Same goes at home too. Whether it's your family or your flatmates who are getting worked up over the latest problem, you simply don't feel the need to get upset, to overreact.

You probably lose your temper incredibly rarely; you hardly ever cry. Traits that make you great in a crisis. You don't just tolerate stress – perhaps you even thrive on it? When everything is hitting the fan, everyone else depends on you. Because you're the one who stays level-headed, keeping your emotions in check and thinking of the best way to get out of a jam.

While some people worry and see threats everywhere around them, you see the world as a benign place. Sure, bad things can happen. But most things turn out OK in the end, so why lose sleep over them? And if something bad happens, you know you can bounce back. After all, it's not like most of the challenges you face are actually going to kill you.

Nor are you the kind of person to dwell on your mistakes or flaws. Sure, you may make a few mistakes and you're not claiming to be perfect at everything, but why fret about anything? Life's too short.

Make the most of yourself – for Low-Resilience people

The modern world rarely confronts us with anything that puts us in mortal peril. But if you're a Low-Resilience individual, your amygdala is hypersensitive all the same. Your early warning system tends to go off a lot, alerting you even to modern-day 'threats', such as looming deadlines or giving a speech in public, the fear of being rejected by someone you like or having to deal with infuriating colleagues.

Even when there's no actual threat to life or limb, your amygdala overreacts, unable to distinguish between a pressing deadline and a hungry animal out to have you for its dinner.

Choose action over avoidance

One way to cope with your overactive amygdala would be to avoid stressful situations. Never speak up at work for fear of ridicule. Never go on a date for fear of rejection. In fact, never set foot outside of the house because of all the terrible things that *could* happen to you. But avoidance – burying your head in the sand and hoping that life will go away – isn't exactly a strategy for success and fulfilment.

Thankfully, science tells us that there is another route. You can inoculate yourself against life's stresses. Doctors inject vaccines, small amounts of harmful viruses, into your body to help it defend itself against the big bad viruses. In exactly the same way, you can immunise yourself against stress by gradual exposure to the very situations that you fear.

Expand your zone of comfort

Do you find yourself avoiding situations in which you think that you might fail, look stupid or be criticised? Perhaps for you it's speaking in public or networking with strangers, confronting a loved one or working through the company finances. It's perfectly understandable to feel scared or put off sometimes. But if you want to grow your confidence and achieve more, you can.

We all have a comfort zone – a certain way of behaving that we feel happy with. The good news is that you can expand your comfort zone.

Every time you step outside of your comfort zone, your reach grows a little. Think of your comfort zone as a circle, with you stood in the middle. Outside of the circle is the zone of uncertainty. 'X' marks the spot where you're standing, feeling comfortable.

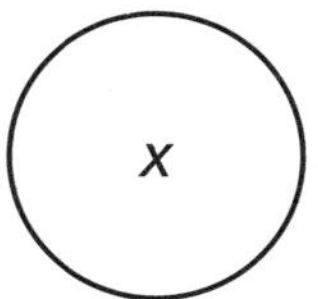

Say you take on a small challenge, taking a tiny step out into the zone of uncertainty. Guess what? Your comfort zone grows to include where you're standing now.

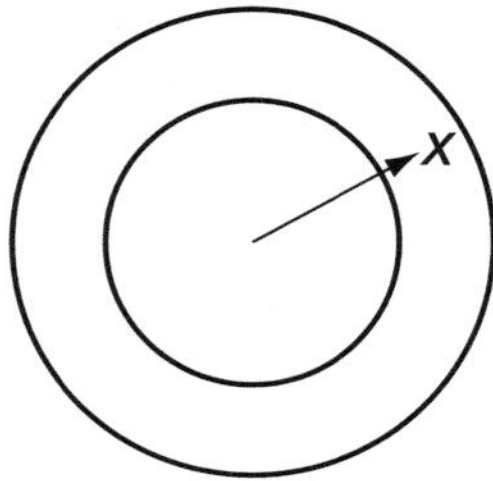

So what happens when you take another step, outside of your *new* comfort zone? Yes, your comfort zone swells even more.

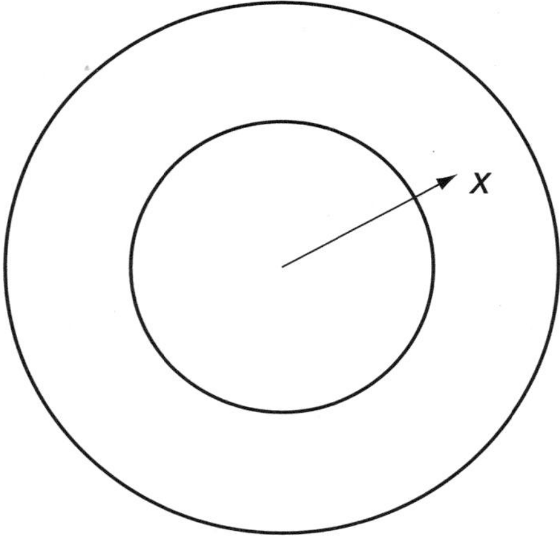

Of course, one huge leap into the unknown would be darned scary, but that's not what I'm saying you should do. Growing your comfort zone is simply a matter of taking a series of small steps, one step at a time. Do that uncomfortable thing a couple of times, and perhaps some more, until it becomes comfortable. Build up your confidence and comfort dealing with a challenge, and then move on. Take on even the tiniest challenge and you grow more courageous when facing the next one. Over time, your comfort zone grows and grows.

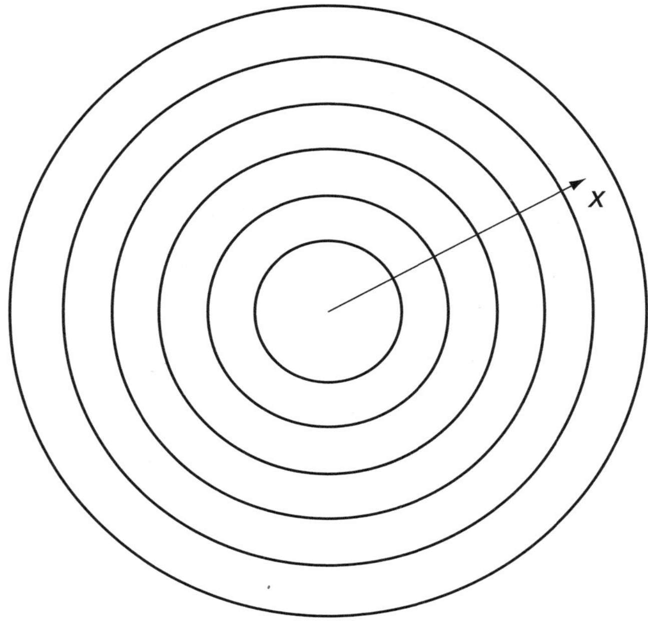

Say you're scared of speaking at your team's annual conference. Why not start by giving a five-minute speech in front of just one supportive buddy? Then add a bit more material and give a ten-minute speech to that same friend. Get that under your belt and move on to giving a speech to two friends. You may have to buy them lunch to persuade them to listen to you, but that's OK. Then maybe give a quick update during your team meeting. By building up in small steps, you grow your confidence to do more.

Over to you

What could be better in your life? In what ways would you like to expand your comfort zone? Jot down three areas of your life in which you'd like to push yourself. We'll come back to these in a later chapter.

- ....
- ....
- ....

Create calm in the storm

Ever had one of those days when you want to scream?

Perhaps it's the threat of an imminent deadline or your boss wants the whole report rewritten *again*. Maybe your babysitter has let you down at short notice when you've got a crucial get-together. Perhaps you simply have too much to do in too little time.

We all have so much to do in our busy lives, so no one can blame you for feeling overwhelmed occasionally. When you're feeling worried or stressed, your productivity falls off the edge of a cliff. The anxious thoughts swirling around your head stop you from thinking rationally. You may blow problems out of proportion, fail to apply your creativity and make mistakes that you wouldn't usually make.

Struggling on when you're stressed is a waste of your time. When you can feel the tension rising, take five minutes to reboot your brain and let your rational operating system reassert control.

Become your best: Taking a time out

When you're worrying or feeling snowed under, you can bet that your amygdala is firing up. But you can quieten it down by performing an easy rote task that allows your higher brain to snatch back control. The key is to persist with the task, ignoring the anxious thoughts that may be trying to pop into your consciousness. Focus your whole attention on the task, concentrating on it as intently as you can. Here are some examples of ways you can override the disruptive emotions running through your head.

- Write in detail about a neutral or pleasant topic – for example, a description of your house or a recent holiday.

- Do some arithmetic – subtract 7 from the number 193 until you reach 0. Either write your answers down or – to challenge yourself further – do it in your head.
- Replay a favourite song in your head. Hear the melody and sing the words in your head from start to finish. Better still, plug into your iPod or even sing out loud if you're alone.
- Take slow, deep breaths. Breathe in through your nose to a slow count of four and breathe out through your mouth to a count of four.
- Pick up a dictionary and write out sentences incorporating words you've never come across before.

Give a name to your emotions

When your emotions feel like a runaway train, an unstoppable juggernaut of anxiety that threatens to derail all rational thought, you *can* put the brakes on.

I recently did a live interview on the BBC's *Working Lunch* programme – a lunchtime business affairs show. Moments before I was due to go on, I was hit by a pang of nerves. My throat went dry and I started coughing. Perhaps because I was going to be on screen with Andy Bond, chief executive officer of mega-retailer Asda. Or maybe it was the thought of speaking live to several million viewers.

But I told myself, 'I feel nervous.' And I asked myself, 'Why?'

Seconds later, I was answering questions on live television and I felt great again.

Cognitive behavioural therapists have known for a long time that quizzing yourself about how you're feeling can help to quell negative emotions. Whether you're feeling depressed over a break-up or angry with a friend who has let you down, you can control your emotions.

Simply name the emotion that you are feeling. Stop whatever else you're doing and say to yourself, 'I feel panicky' or 'I am feeling guilty' or 'I am feeling . . .' whatever else you may be feeling.

Become your best: FADE tension away

Naming the emotion you're feeling is a start, but you can do much more. This is a shortened version of a technique from my book, *Confidence: The art of getting whatever you want* (Prentice Hall, 2008). To get the most out of this technique, grab a pen and paper and take 60 seconds to *write down* your thoughts:

- **Feelings.** Name all of the moods and emotions that you're feeling. Write down, 'I am feeling . . .' – sad, jealous, afraid, resentful, uncertain – all of the emotions you feel.
- **Actions.** Write down how your feelings are affecting your actions, your behaviour. Are your hands trembling? Are you close to throwing in the towel or bursting into tears?
- **Defects.** Quiz your feelings and actions and ask yourself if they're appropriate and productive. Imagine your best friend is giving you advice – what would he or she say about how you're feeling and behaving?
- **Evaluate your feelings again.** Ask yourself how you're feeling now. Do you feel better?

How you feel and behave is determined by a constant battle between your rational and emotional minds – the higher brain versus the lower brain. The mere act of naming the emotions you're feeling can begin to calm an unruly amygdala. The more you quiz the turmoil in your head, the better you feel. Going through the mental rigour of analysing your feelings allows your rational side to begin to conquering your emotions.

But you have to *do* it to get the benefits. Understanding how the technique might work in theory is *not* the same as putting it into practice. You have been warned!

Improve your persuasiveness

How many times do you tell your colleagues what's great about their ideas or compliment your loved ones? How often do you point out the positives in a situation before discussing the negatives?

You have a particular gift, which is to sense what *could* go wrong. While High-Resilience people blithely overlook potential problems, you're good at putting bad ideas out of their misery. That means, however, you may be seen by people – colleagues, clients, friends and family, your boss – as unsupportive, too negative, overly critical, unnecessarily pessimistic.

To make sure that *I'm* not being too harsh, I asked for a second opinion. Angela Mansi is a highly regarded coach and a senior lecturer at Westminster Business School. She has a similar warning:

> *You are highly alert to potential threats and problems, which can be a strength, but being too focused on these means you might fail to see the positive aspects of new situations. Certainly, others may see you as overly critical.*

You don't see yourself as a pessimist – only a realist. You see the world how it really is and not through the rose-tinted spectacles that others see it through. Only problem is, the rest of the world doesn't appreciate a critic.

Think about it for a moment. Who are the people you value most in life? Are they the ones who support you, help you to focus on the positives and make you feel good? Or the ones who remind you of your flaws, tell you about your mistakes and point out how your plans won't work?

No matter how good your intentions when you point out problems, I guarantee you that few people will thank you for doing it. People shun critics like they shun the arrogant office bore. People start to see you as the killjoy, the one with the 'can't do' attitude. They begin to expect the words coming from your mouth to be critical or disapproving, so why bother to listen at all?

I'm not saying you should pretend to be a sunny person who sees only sweetness and light in the world. All you have to do is stop making negative comments and start asking questions. Rather than pointing out problems, look for solutions.

How much positivity is enough?

Emeritus Professor John Gottman at the University of Washington has spent decades analysing married couples and he's found that he can predict with 90 per cent certainty whether a couple will divorce or still be together ten years later. His finding? That flourishing couples make positive statements five times as often as they make negative comments. In contrast, couples that later ended up hitting the divorce courts made only one positive comment for every negative comment.

Similar work has looked at successful teams and their less successful counterparts too. Researcher Marcial Losada compared high-performing work teams to teams that were less successful. After observing 15 such teams, he found that high-performing teams tended to make *three times* more positive than negative comments, whereas less successful teams made far fewer positive comments for every negative comment.

Avoid negative language, such as 'But . . .', 'I can't see how . . .', 'I doubt it' or 'That won't work because . . .' Instead, replace it with constructive questions that stimulate further debate and make people think:

- 'That's a fascinating idea. How would that work?'
- 'Let's brainstorm ideas as to how we can ...'
- 'That's an interesting idea. I think it will exceed our budget, but what else could we cut back on if we want to do this?'
- 'What if we ...?'
- 'Are there other ways of looking at this?'

Reprogram your perspective

What do you pay attention to? I never used to notice dogs until our household gained a dog over the summer. He's a schnauzer and we've called him Byron. Now that we have him, I notice dogs everywhere and I seem to spot different schnauzers at least a couple of times a week.

So what's changed? Are there suddenly more dogs – particularly schnauzers – in my part of town? Or is it that my perspective is now more attuned to dogs?

We all respond to the world not as it is but according to the way we perceive it. You can tweak your perspective depending on what you look for.

Two people can see the same circumstances as either a disaster or an opportunity. I recently worked with a large group of managers who had been made redundant. Many of them had been working for the company for over ten years, but the new owners of the organisation decided to shut down the entire department. I was brought in to offer 'outplacement counselling' – practical support with CVs and interview techniques to help them find new jobs as quickly as possible.

Some of the managers were upset. Several had voices clogged with emotion; a few were on the verge of tears. Quite a few of the hardiest managers, though, saw it as an opportunity. One manager, Neil, said that he'd been doing the job for far too long anyway. He saw it as a chance to do something fresh. For many years, he'd been toying with working in forestry and land conservation. Another, Georgiana, was intrigued by the idea of life coaching, of helping others to find their way through difficult times.

Whatever your current outlook on life – whether it's pretty neutral or extremely pessimistic – you can reprogram your perspective. Noticing the negatives in life is nothing more than a bad habit that people fall into. High-Resilience people edit out their failures and concentrate on their successes. So can you.

Become your best: Looking for positives

This is a simple yet incredibly powerful technique for calming your unruly amygdala. Buy a diary and, at the end of each day, write down *at least* three successes, achievements or positive moments. Perhaps it's the comment you made in a meeting that made a colleague nod in agreement. Maybe it's the fact that you complimented a friend on a new outfit and made her feel good. Or simply that you got to work early enough to enjoy a coffee and muffin while reading the newspaper before the first meeting of the day.

High-Resilience people play back successes big and small all the time. They replay them, share them with anyone who'll listen and keep mulling them over and over again. No wonder they have such a confident mindset: they focus so tenaciously on their triumphs.

So look for your successes. Anything. The only criterion for inclusion in your list is that it's important to *you*. And when you start to look out for three a day, you may often find that your list runs on and on.

You can *choose* to feel revitalised rather than run down. It really is up to you.

I've been working with Ewan, who started using this technique. He sent me an email saying, 'On trying this exercise the other evening, I noticed so many things to be pleased about! It goes to show that we can unwittingly neglect the positives in life, only noticing the negatives.'

When you start to see things differently, you think differently, you feel differently, you act differently. Looking for three or more successes a day will only take a few minutes. Remember what I said in Chapter 1 – that many of the techniques in this book are small tweaks that get big results? This is one of them. In fact, the University of Pennsylvania's Professor Martin Seligman, one of the world's top psychologists, found that using the 'three good things' trick for as little as seven days helped to reduce worry and anxiety for up to six months. Pretty amazing, right?

Learn to let go

> "Grant me the serenity to accept the things I cannot change,
>
> Courage to change the things I can,
>
> And the wisdom to know the difference."
>
> **Reinhold Niebuhr, pastor**

Worry is constructive if it spurs you into action, if it makes you prepare for a situation, deal with its aftermath or put in place preventative measures for the future. But worry can be destructive if it merely dwells in your thoughts, causes your mood to plummet and stops you from getting on with your life.

So focus on what you can change and forget the rest.

If an issue is preying on your mind, set aside a limited amount of time to worry about it. Allow yourself say 10 or 20 minutes to think about it and make plans. What can you do about it today? What actions should you get down on a piece of paper to do tomorrow or next week? Who can you talk to about it?

Once you've done that, let the matter go. Move on to a different activity, a new task. Let go as if you're a positive person and you may eventually become positive and confident to boot.

Make the most of yourself – for High-Resilience people

If you are High-Resilience, you are the envy of many people. When people around you are panicking and saying, 'It'll never work', you forge on regardless. You shake off criticism and negativity. And even when things do go wrong, you bounce back so, so quickly. All this means that you come across as self-assured, poised, confident.

But that very self-belief can be double-edged. Others may wrongly interpret your confidence as arrogance. I'm sure you *don't* think that you're better than other people, but others may feel you inadvertently shrug off criticisms that are actually worth hearing. So the question is: do you ask for *enough* feedback and take on board *sufficient* criticism to keep your life and career on track?

See yourself as others see you

I read somewhere that one of the executives at the Oracle Corporation, a software company in California, once said of his CEO Larry Ellison, 'The difference between Larry Ellison and God is that God doesn't believe he is Larry Ellison.'

This is very amusing, but you can see how there's a fine line between confidence and being seen by other people as arrogant. Between shrugging off unhelpful, negative comments and ignoring constructive criticism.

When was the last time you were on the receiving end of criticism that changed the way you behave?

I helped the managing director of a mobile phone manufacturer to interview a handful of candidates for the position of sales director. The MD wanted to hire someone who could take constructive criticism. So I asked all of the candidates the same three-part question: 'When was the last time you were criticised? What did that person say? What did you do about it?'

One of the candidates, a charismatic manager with over 20 years' experience of corporate sales, struggled with the question. 'I can't remember a recent time.' So I rephrased the question and asked, 'When was the last time you made a mistake? Could you tell me about that?'

Another pause. He finally came up with an example – that had transpired five years ago.

He honestly believed that he hadn't been criticised or made a mistake in five years! That didn't surprise me though. I had asked all of the candidates to complete a personality test and his results showed he had extremely high levels of Resilience.

No one is perfect. No one is so good at their job and marriage, pastimes and friendships that they are above criticism. High achievers intentionally seek out feedback. They are hungry to hear the bad news. They see criticism as a gift rather than a burden because it allows them to understand their blind spots and fix their flaws.

People don't always tell you what they're thinking. Just because they don't *say* anything doesn't mean they wouldn't like you to change. So make it a habit to seek feedback from the key people in your life. When a project is over, ask colleagues or customers what you could have done better. Ask your boss once every month or two how you could do your job better. Ask your partner how you could be more helpful around the house or a better parent.

Become your best: Ask for the truth, the whole truth

So many people can't take criticism – they go ballistic or sulk when they receive feedback on how they're doing. Unsurprisingly then, many of the people in your life won't want to give you honest feedback. Apart from your boss and perhaps your partner, most of them would rather give you positive strokes than incisive feedback about what you don't do so well. Even if you beg for candid opinions, you're probably going to get sugar-coated answers.

The best way to find out what people really think of you and how you could improve is to ask for *anonymous* feedback. Ask a dozen people who know you well to write letters to you. Tell them to *type* the letters and send them to you anonymously. Knowing that they won't have to deliver bad news to your face, you may get a much franker picture of how you come across.

Choose your own questions or ask the following:

- What do I do well that I should not change?
- Are there any aspects of myself that I have trouble seeing?
- What could I do differently to be more effective?

When you receive the replies, be sure to look at the common themes. *One* person mentioning an issue may not be a big deal, but if two or three people mention it, you'd better take notice.

Give thanks for a poke in the eye

Once upon a time, the chairman and owner of a consulting firm that I worked for – I'll call him Jeremy – decided that we should all give each other written feedback. We each chose four people and asked them to give us feedback on three questions:

- What good behaviours should I *start* doing?
- What bad behaviours should I *stop* doing?

- What good behaviours do I already do that I should *continue* doing?

I found the exercise incredibly instructive. This was way back in the early days of my career and I'd never received such blunt, honest opinions. I didn't like a lot of what I read about myself. But I decided that if someone had written it to me, it was probably true. (I now use this *start, stop, continue* framework a lot in my work. You could do worse than adopt it too.)

At the same time as I got feedback on me, several senior people asked me for upward feedback. And two stood out. One of them, Kathleen, stopped me in the corridor and said: 'Rob, I realise you've only been working here for a few months, so I appreciate you sticking your neck out to tell me what you really think. Thank you.'

Jeremy set up a formal meeting in which he spent an hour telling me why I'd got the wrong end of the stick. He used phrases such as 'What you don't understand is that . . .' and 'What you don't see is that I do actually . . .' He discounted or rationalised every comment I had made about him. Duly chastened, I learned never to criticise him again.

But what's more fascinating is what happened to Kathleen. She eventually left the firm to found a business that is now several times larger than Jeremy's. I'm convinced that at least part of her success was down to her willingness to take on board constructive criticism. The lesson: be more like Kathleen, less like Jeremy.

Become your best: Accept feedback with good grace

Say you receive feedback that is a shock – awful, disappointing, completely unexpected. You don't agree with any of it. How should you respond?

The only response you should give is to say, 'Thank you.'

Nothing more. Those two short words show your appreciation for the fact that people have taken the trouble to give you honest feedback.

Avoid at all costs trying to explain your behaviour. You don't have to take the feedback on board – you can ignore it if you like – but don't try to argue or justify yourself. No matter how you dress it up, your words will sound like excuses.

When someone offers you their opinion, what they are thinking is, 'Here's what I think you can do differently,' not 'I wonder why you are the way you are.' You have to respect the fact that other people have the right to an opinion, no matter how badly they may have misunderstood the situation or misinterpreted your actions. So don't try to explain how the situation arose. Don't talk about extenuating circumstances or that they don't understand the pressure you're under.

No matter how softly you couch it, saying anything other than 'thank you' cuts off future constructive criticism. And I can guarantee that you will only come across as defensive or in denial. As sassy best friends sometimes say in the movies, 'De-nial ain't just a river in Egypt, honey.'

So. Shut up. Listen. Swallow your objections. Say 'thank you' or, if you must say more, say something like, 'Thank you. That's a lot to take on board, but I will give it some thought and see what I can learn from it.'

Enough lecturing. Now go put it into practice.

Show that you care

I coached a banking executive who was the poster boy for High-Resilience. Calm, cool and superbly collected, he never lost his temper or let the pressure of work get to him. I asked him if this was ever a problem and he said that it wasn't.

'Oh, but my wife *hates* it,' he conceded after a little thought. 'When she's annoyed about something, she'll yell at me and want a response. But I go quiet and let her get it off her chest. The fact that I won't argue back makes her even angrier. She accuses me of bottling up my emotions, of refusing to say what I think. I'm not. She can't understand that nothing ever bothers me enough to get worked up.'

If you're a High-Resilience individual, you must understand that you are in some ways unusual. *You* may hardly ever feel stressed, but *most* other people experience more stress than you. Seriously. Very little gets to you, whereas a lot more bothers the people around you.

If you're not careful, you could come across as emotionless, unfeeling – like the cold and calculating Mr Spock on the Starship Enterprise. So don't be too quick to dismiss the predicaments that other people face. To you it may seem trivial or eminently fixable, but to them it may seem like the end of the world. Reading the sections within this chapter on how Low-Resilience people see the world may help you to appreciate their side of the story. Be sure to show that you care, that you understand – even if you can't personally imagine what the fuss is all about.

ONWARDS AND UPWARDS

Remember again that Resilience – like all of the personality dimensions – is a continuum. Yes, a score of 16 may put you into the High-Resilience category, but even more so if you score 18 or 20. The same goes for Low-Resilience scores too – 6 may be low, but 2 or 0 is very low.

So you may be either high or low on the scale. You can be very high or very low – or a blend of the two. To help you remember the broad differences, here's a brief summary of words and phrases that distinguish Low-Resilience from High-Resilience.

Low-Resilience	**High-Resilience**
More tense and worried than they like.	Usually calm, composed.
Spot problems in situations.	See only opportunities.
Very critical of own performance.	Not very critical of own performance.
Sensitive to hazards and danger.	May not notice hazards and danger.
Agonise over mistakes and setbacks.	Bounce back quickly.
Take on board negative feedback.	May not seek out enough negative feedback.

If you scored lower on Resilience:

- Look for gradual ways to expand your comfort zone. Avoidance isn't a strategy. Courage fuels itself – be sure to take small, courageous actions every day.
- Take time out and analyse your feelings when stress is getting on top of you. Look for the positives at the end of every day. Negativity is nothing more than a bad habit that you can reprogram.
- Your effectiveness with other people is governed by how they see you. Aim to ask questions rather than point out problems so that other people find you less negative.
- Have a look at another of my books, *Confidence: The art of getting whatever you want* (Prentice Hall, 2008) – it's packed with a ton of other tools and techniques like these if you want to take your confidence up, up and away!

If you scored higher on Resilience:

- Make regular efforts to gather feedback on what you could do better. Just because people don't *tell* you doesn't mean they think you're perfect!
- Accept that other people may see you differently from how you see yourself. Respect the fact that they are entitled to their point of view. You need only say 'thank you' for any feedback: trying to explain your point of view could make you appear defensive.
- As so little bothers you, be careful not to come across as cold and unfeeling. Read the descriptions of how Low-Resilience people experience the world and try to get a glimpse into their concerns.

04

Affiliation

"Treasure your relationships, not your possessions."

Anthony J. D'Angelo, writer

Technology is pretty amazing, isn't it? If you want to get in touch with someone, you can send an email or call on the office phone, the home phone, the mobile phone. Maybe see each other via a video link or using a webcam. Even send an instant message on MSN Messenger, 'poke' each other on Facebook or update your Twitter feed about what you're up to. The list goes on.

Yet humans evolved to deal with each other face to face, eye to eye. We're social animals. We have an in-built need to get together, to shake hands, hug, kiss, pat each other on the back, whisper in each other's ears. We actually have centres in our brains that are specifically designed to recognise human faces – that part of the brain lights up whenever we see a friendly face.

But we don't all need people to the same extent. You probably know some people who are never at home, who are constantly going to parties and evenings out, socialising and networking with friends, colleagues and clients. Even when they're at home, they're entertaining, having friends round for drinks, dinners or to watch the big match together.

You probably also know people who prefer to keep to themselves, who shy away from the spotlight and prefer the company of their good friends rather than constantly having to meet different people.

These two extremes represent the two ends of the Affiliation dimension – the extent to which you enjoy and are energised by spending time with people. You probably already have a very good sense of where you sit on that continuum.

Your Affiliation

Go back to Questionnaire 3 on page 8. Award yourself two points each time you ticked 'Agree' for any of the following statements: 1, 2, 4, 7 and 8. Give yourself two points each time you ticked 'Disagree' for any of the following statements: 3, 5, 6, 9 and 10. You should have a total score between 0 and 20.

A score of 8 or less suggests that you have a low level on Affiliation. A score of 10 or 12 suggests that you're somewhere in the middle, possessing average levels on Affiliation. A score of 14 or more suggests that you have a high level on Affiliation.

But where would *you* put yourself on the Affiliation spectrum? Remember that your score is only a rough guide to your true personality. Does one or the other end of the spectrum resonate more strongly with you? Where would your dearest friends put you?

Remember that both low scores *and* high scores have their own strengths and shortcomings. But you only need to read the sections that are aimed at your personality profile. If your score was average for Affiliation, read both sets of descriptions and cherry-pick the advice that seems most relevant to you.

What kind of person are you?

You're probably already familiar with the concept of the Affiliation dimension and the two ends of its spectrum. Low-Affiliation individuals are naturally more introverted: High-Affiliation people are essentially more extroverted.

Our natural levels of Affiliation are down to how much buzz – or, to be more precise, physiological arousal – we have in our brains. Individuals who are low for Affiliation have plenty of internal buzz, so don't seek much stimulation from other people. Individuals who are higher for Affiliation may have less buzz in their brains and so look for ways to gain that energy from the people around them.

The Low-Affiliation person: self-sufficient and independent

You're the kind of person who enjoys your time alone because you get to produce your best work. You can think, muse and reflect.

It's not that you lack social skills, you just take pleasure in having your own space. You find being with people for too long somewhat draining. They disrupt your train of thought, bugging and bothering you with questions, comments, noise. They prevent you from doing the stuff that needs doing. Getting away from them allows you to recharge. In a way, you are your own best companion.

You do not necessarily shy away from meeting new people. Plus, you're a great listener – you don't feel the need to talk about yourself and monopolise the conversation all the time. You simply prefer to spend time with your circle of closest friends. You take more pleasure from getting to know a smaller group of people intimately than in flitting from one new person to the next. Perhaps you shun the superficial quality of those kinds of interactions.

When you have work to do, you can get your head down and focus ruthlessly on it. You thrive when you can work on your own or with a smaller group of people rather than an endless procession of new faces. You enjoy the technical and mental challenges of your work.

You don't get distracted easily. You don't wonder what other people are doing or get drawn into idle conversation and gossip. The work won't do itself, right?

The High-Affiliation person: the unreserved extrovert

You're drawn to people, like a moth to a flame – you can't help yourself. You probably find yourself striking up conversations with complete strangers on trains and planes or when you're caught in a boring queue. If you see someone wearing something you admire or doing something you're intrigued by, you have no compunction about talking to them. When you interact with others, you feel alive. You find it easy to smile and love to laugh. People say that you're approachable, gregarious, outgoing, sociable, talkative, even entertaining.

Hell for you would be a job in which you were stuck in front of a computer with no one to talk to. You do your best work when you're surrounded by people. When you can bounce ideas around, talk things through and share your thoughts there and then. Why send an email when you can speak to someone face to face?

You enjoy connecting with people, forging relationships. Others may shy away from meeting new people, but not you. You find new faces a challenge – you want to strike up conversations and see what you have in common. Fun for you is a roomful of people that you can delight and charm.

You're happy to share information about yourself, your work, your loves and losses, and your life. You sometimes end up being the centre of attention when you get together with friends or colleagues. You don't mean for it to happen, it just does.

Make the most of yourself – for Low-Affiliation people

As someone who appreciates having your space, you enjoy thinking, working and being on your own. Thing is, even the most independent of us need other people occasionally.

Imagine that someone phones you up. You met once, briefly, at a party about six months ago. You're slightly surprised to hear from him, but you chat for a bit and he tells you that he and his wife have three kids. You didn't know he had children – you obviously didn't talk for very long at that party. He asks you a couple of questions. How are you doing? Up to much? Then he asks, 'Er, I was wondering if you could babysit little Thomas on Saturday night?'

How would you feel?

I don't know about you, but most people I've posed this scenario to say they'd be more than a little annoyed. That this person is taking advantage. So most people would say no to the request from the 'friend'.

Let's flip the situation now. Say you're asking a neighbour or a colleague to help you out. *You* feel that the request is perfectly sensible, but does your neighbour or colleague see it the same way? Your colleague is probably busy and may have other people asking for help. Does he see you as a buddy or merely someone who works at the same place? Same goes for your neighbour. Does she see you as a friend she can chat to and rely on or simply a person who happens to share the same geography?

You're probably reading this book because you want to achieve more in life. Well, the truth is that we need people; we need relationships to succeed and we must build those relationships *before* we need them. If we go to people *only* to seek their help, we come across as desperate, as beggars – just people they know, not true friends. Why should they help you when they could be helping their friends?

Understanding the power of relationships

Fact: people with more friends make more money. OK, money isn't everything. So here's another fact: people who have more friendships tend to live longer than those with fewer friends. Yes, it's official. Scientists and health experts tell us that people who engage in more social interaction not only have a longer life expectancy but also tend to be healthier. Perhaps having a circle of friends means that people can bring you chicken soup when you're ill or provide a sympathetic ear when you're feeling down.

Having more people in your life won't just help you to achieve your goals. It'll keep you healthy and alive for longer too.

The good news is that you can build rock-solid relationships. No matter how few or how many friends you have, you can gather more. One research study tells us that both extroverts and introverts can be good salespeople. However, introverts have to *behave* like extroverts in order to succeed. If some people can do it, why not you too?

Understand human nature

Suppose you receive an email from a customer that starts, 'I don't suppose you've dispatched my order yet.' What *exactly* does he mean? Is he a little annoyed or downright angry? Being sarcastic or merely playful? Or is he trying to say that he understands you're busy? Without tone of voice to guide us, we can easily reach the wrong conclusions.

Now reverse the situation. Because if you're sending lots of emails, you can be certain that it's your clients, colleagues and friends who will be wondering exactly what *you* mean.

When we can see someone face to face, we can pick up all sorts of clues that tell us what to say next. When a friend cringes or blushes, we know to shy away from a topic. When a client stays silent but nods approvingly, we know we're on the right track. You can't get any of that by email or even over the phone.

Humans have always been a social species. Since the dawn of recorded history, humans have clumped together in tribes. So our brains evolved to derive pleasure from the company of people we trust. And we tend to trust the people we're near. This is because skin-on-skin contact – even in the form of something as simple as a handshake – releases oxytocin in the brain, a hormone that bonds people together. A mother cradling her baby receives a chemical hit of oxytocin. You get a boost of oxytocin when someone wraps you up in a bear hug, making you feel safe and loved when you've had a bad day. You can't shake hands or exchange social kisses by email. You can't give a hug or a pat on the back over the phone.

The most successful endeavours come about through cooperation, collaboration and teamwork. Whether at work or at home, you need to connect with people.

Press the flesh

If you're a Low-Affiliation individual, you probably feel quite comfortable communicating via technology – email, phone calls and personal digital assistants (PDAs). But you must realise that other people need more.

To develop stronger relationships, to build that sense of liking and rapport, you need to meet more people in person. Make a conscious effort to get together more frequently than you feel you should. Because people who meet up get to know each other better. They like each other more and can't help but want to do well by each other.

Thomas McConnell, an IT skills trainer, tells me:

> *Although I like to believe that, with me, what you see is what you get, I've realised that I need to connect more with clients. My natural inclination is to do everything by email, but clients like to put a face to a name. I've learned that meeting up is as much about chatting about nothing in particular and bonding as it is about exchanging information.*
>
> *I caught up with one client to discuss amendments to a training manual we're writing. We could have done it by phone or email, but as we chatted we happened to stray on to what else we're up to. We threw ideas around and came up with a new project that will keep me employed for another three months.*

I'm not asking you to create new friendships and relationships from nothing. Only to make an effort to spend more time with people who could enrich your work and life. Rather than telephoning a colleague on another floor, wander over and see if she can spare five minutes to talk your project through. Rather than having an email conversation with a friend about your favourite television programme, arrange to meet up and watch it together.

Back in the 1980s, management guru Tom Peters gave this idea a name in the workplace: MBWA – 'Management By Walking Around'. That was in the days before email, the mobile phone, the Internet – the need is even more pressing in today's world. And it's not just the office where it counts. I therefore suggest a new acronym: SBMU – 'Success By Meeting Up'. Whatever your aims in life, you will have a better chance at achieving them if you meet up (in the flesh) with others.

Technology helps us to shuffle facts and information around at digital speeds, but true relationship building is a contact sport.

Over to you

Who should you spend more time with? Take five minutes right now to consider:

- Who are the most crucial dozen (or more) people who can affect your professional and personal goals and your physical and mental well-being? Perhaps they are key customers if you run a business, or your editors if you're a freelance writer. Maybe they are a group of colleagues in other departments, on whom you depend to do your job well. Or simply friends who can help you stick with a diet or the in-laws because they could pick your kids up from school. Whoever they are, make a note of them. As these people are so important, you must never take them for granted.

- How can you strengthen your ties with these key people? Maybe it's dropping by for lunch, a coffee, an after-work drink or a breakfast meeting. Perhaps to see an exhibition or indulge in being armchair fans of your favourite sport one weekend. Different people have different interests. So what's the best way to spend some time with each individual you've highlighted?
- How will you bring up the subject? If you get at all nervous about broaching such conversations, rehearse what you want to say, as you would for a job interview.
- When will you do it? Set yourself a deadline for arranging to meet with these key people.

I'll give you a tiny example of how you can get started. Most people are too busy to take a proper lunch break. But change how you see your lunchtime. Instead of thinking of it as an intrusion into your day, see it as an opportunity to cement a relationship and remind people that you exist. Even if it's merely popping out for 15 minutes to grab a sandwich together, make sure to do it with different people as often as you can.

Understand the need for networking

I answer questions as a business adviser on the website www.management-issues.com. One reader wrote:

> *I've never been the world's most social person but I recently joined a new company where social networking seems almost as important as the job itself. I'd much rather get back to the wife and kids and it's a long drive home. Any advice would be appreciated.*

This was my reply:

> *Success in many organisations often comes down to social relationships. If your colleagues are socialising, they are building bridges and*

getting to know each other personally. And knowing someone personally is only a short step away from promoting them or entrusting them with that glamorous project overseas. Think about it: if you had to promote one of two people who were more or less equally qualified for a job but one of them was your best friend, who would you promote?

Outside of the workplace, Hilary Cottam, a founder of social welfare organisation Participle, believes that networking can help the elderly: 'Many seniors worry about their safety, losing their money and what to do when the heating breaks down. The secret of a happy old age is getting on top of the everyday and being networked.' Strong networks may benefit disenfranchised young people too. She writes on her website, 'Behind every thriving young person is a personal support network: parents, family members, friends, teachers, pastors and so on.'

From young to old, from personal to professional, the secret of success lies in the fact that people want to help out people they *like*. If people don't know you, how can they warm to you and want to help you out? When you have formal meetings with people, their defences are up; they're sceptical and wary. It's often when you're chatting about nothing in particular, when you're most relaxed, that you end up striking deals and getting friends and colleagues to offer advice and assistance. Whatever your goals, you need a network of people who like you.

If you're looking for a job, you can ask friends to look out for opportunities, look over your CV, introduce you to the right people, run through mock interviews and give you advice. If you hanker after the boss's job, your network can guide you, warn you about difficult colleagues, give you the inside scoop versus the official line and put a good word in with your boss. Even if you're only looking for a good plumber or decorator for your home, would you rather look for one at random in the *Yellow Pages* or talk to the people you know and get a recommendation from someone you trust?

Over to you

In what ways could a network help you? Write down three ways in which either a personal or professional network could help you.

- ....
- ....
- ....

Get used to using people power

Networking and socialising at work aren't simply distractions from the 'real work' of your job. I sometimes hear comments such as: 'I don't have enough time to do the job I'm paid for, let alone waste precious time trying to widen my circle of acquaintances.' Ah, but focusing only on what you need to do today can blind you to the larger problems or opportunities that could come your way.

John Whiting, a partner at the world's largest professional services firm PricewaterhouseCoopers, tells me:

> *Of course you have to do your daily work, but many projects are too large and complex for just one person to deliver. Even if you're very good at your job, you can't know everything. Whether you work for a large firm or you're on your own, sooner or later an issue will come up that you need help on. So you need people around you as back-up, a network. And for that you have to do some reaching out.*

You can bounce ideas around with people in your network, cross-pollinate and test ideas. You can share information and insights, seek referrals and recommendations, even get moral support when times are tough. Whether you're a small business owner on the lookout for new customers, a manager trying to make things happen, a parent looking for parenting advice or a retiree looking for ways to keep your mind sharp, networking is a fundamental part of succeeding in the twenty-first century.

If they can do it . . .

I worked with Leonard, a manager at an insurance brokerage, who found it difficult to relate to his team. He had received feedback that his team found him somewhat detached and unapproachable. His preference was to sit in his office, dealing with his people only at certain hours of the day or in formal meetings.

I encouraged him to spend more time roaming around the desks of his team, chatting. I suggested he do this for 15 minutes at some point in the morning, 15 minutes at lunchtime and a further 15 minutes in the afternoon – only 45 minutes a day. I emphasised that, because it didn't come naturally to him, he would have to make it a task to tick off his 'to do' list every day.

I told him that it didn't matter what he talked about. In fact, he would do better to talk about his team's personal interests – their children, the football scores, what was on TV or, in fact, anything other than the work itself.

At first he struggled, but after a few months he found it easier. He noticed that people felt more at ease with him too. They came to him earlier with ideas and issues, allowing the team to work together more effectively.

Because social chit-chat didn't come spontaneously to him, we turned it into an objective, a daily goal. By monitoring and measuring his own performance, he developed the kind of rapport that allowed him to lead his team properly for the first time.

Grow the number of people in your address book

Networking is both one of the most important and one of the most dreaded challenges facing people who want to achieve more. Thankfully, it's also terribly misunderstood. It's actually a lot easier than you think.

You may associate networking with milling about at conferences, trying to strike up conversations with complete strangers, stumbling to find common ground and pushing business cards at each other. But that's so last season.

Networking is simply about creating relationships with people. Perhaps the best way to describe networking is that it's about making friends – it should be called 'net*friending*' rather than networking. Ultimately, you may wish to discuss work or exchange ideas and advice with them. But the first step is simply to have a conversation, to say 'hello'.

Ever asked a friend to go for lunch or a drink? If you have, then you already have all the skills you need to network. Networking is simply socialising, growing your circle of friends.

Over to you

Want to get started in a small way? You probably have certain people you have lunch, coffee or drinks with. Next time, I'd like you to wander over to your friend's desk and, instead of only inviting your friend out, invite the person your friend sits next to as well.

'Hey, John – fancy a bite to eat? Actually, Alison, would you like to come with us too? We're going to grab a sandwich from that place across the street.'

Not so difficult, right?

Extend your reach far and wide

OK, so growing your network isn't that harrowing, but I am often asked by managers and would-be entrepreneurs how they can meet more *senior* people. Here's the good news: you *don't* have to attend conferences and cocktail parties. One of the best tactics, as a networker in training, is to turn your personal interests into ways to meet people.

At a major accountancy firm, Joanne Croft wanted to build her network, but didn't know how. Talking it through, she mentioned, with a little frustration, that there were only men's football and rugby teams within the firm. So she put a notice on the company's intranet asking if anyone would be willing to put together a women's netball team. She found several dozen women willing to take part on at least an occasional basis. In the last year, the team has challenged similar teams from other firms, including lawyers and bankers. To make up numbers, the team has often had to draft in friends of friends, which has only added to the diversity and value of the network. What began as a sporting enterprise has coalesced into a surprisingly powerful network of women spread across not only the divisions and departments of the firm but also other organisations.

Even your personal attributes, such as your nationality, gender, sexuality, religion or political leanings, can prove fertile ground for building a network. If you want to grow your network, you only need to think about what you might have in common with people.

Become your best: Turning your interests into pots of gold

To grow your network, join sports teams, voluntary or charity groups, clubs and community groups. Get involved in a cause – a charity, the environment, the committee of a relevant professional or business association. If you can't find a group to join, why not start one – based perhaps on a shared interest, your religion, your gender and so on? At work, look also to join interdepartmental projects or cross-functional teams.

Having a mutual goal or something at stake is a great way for people to bond. Perhaps it's raising £10,000 for charity, winning an award, bringing in a project on time and under budget, or beating a competitor. Whether the group ultimately celebrates success or commiserates over disappointment, you get to bond and know each other better.

You may be surprised at how many people would love to get involved in sports, community activities, and interest groups – they're just waiting for someone to ask them. And that someone could be you.

Nurture your network

Great, so you can grow your network now. But be aware that your network is a living, breathing entity – it needs tending and feeding to flourish.

Helen McNamara, marketing expert at SME Academy, tells me:

> *People are so busy that they forget about you. After meeting someone, it takes between five and seven points of contact to build trust and for people to remember you. You need to drip-feed contact with them so you become the first person they think of, whether you're promoting yourself, your company, or whatever else.*

Simply having names and phone numbers in your address book is not the same as having a network! You need to keep a hum of conversation going with people *before* you need them. One of the biggest mistakes would-be networkers make is to call on people within their networks *only* when they need them. But if you wait until you need people, such a call can smack of desperation and risk alienating people with whom you have only a passing relationship.

Become your best: Using the principle of reciprocity

Human beings are programmed to repay favours. Buy someone a drink and you'll get one in return. Give free samples out at a supermarket and customers are more likely to buy that product. Make a concession during a negotiation and the opposition feels obliged to return the gesture.

The more you can help the people in your network, the stronger your relationships with them will become. That's the way our brains work. When you help people, they feel a deep-seated desire to help you out too.

It doesn't have to be in huge ways. I'm not talking about taking the week off to repair the roof on a friend's house or sacrificing your prospects of promotion to clear the way for a colleague. Think about all the small ways in which you can show people that you're willing to help out, that you care.

Send them articles that might be of interest or a text message asking how that big meeting went. Perhaps email the link to a review of a film they're wondering about or a book they're thinking of buying. Offer to proofread a report they're writing or to drop off their dry cleaning as you're popping that way anyhow. Congratulate them on a job change or a new family arrival. Every little thing helps to cement your relationships.

Take a few moments right now to think of something that you can do for ten people in your life.

There are plenty of ways to keep that hum going within your network. For example, one of my clients, Anne-Marie Lindley, writes a restaurant review blog. Every two or three weeks, she invites a group of between six and eight people to dine with her on the pretext of judging the restaurant. The blog is a hobby – she doesn't care how many readers she attracts. But it does serve as a compelling way to draw groups of unrelated people together.

A friend, Justin Goldberg, sets up lunches and after-work drinks for people who might be able to help each other. For example, he invited me to have a drink with him and a business journalist.

As a corporate psychologist, I can come up with ideas for the journalist to write about. In return, the journalist can publicise the work that my colleagues and I do at Talentspace.

A network is, by definition, a lattice of people, a muddle of cross-connections. Why compartmentalise your colleagues, friends or acquaintances? If you introduce people to each other, they have no choice but to talk about you whenever they get together!

Over to you

Who could you introduce to each other right now? Consider not only people who could benefit from knowing each other but also people who might simply enjoy meeting each other. Write down three pairs of people that you will commit to introducing to each other within the next month.

- ....
- ....
- ....

Pledge to send an email or call to suggest that the three of you (because you need to be there too!) meet for a drink, breakfast, game of tennis, whatever. Then keep doing it. Make it a regular commitment to get pairs or even small groups of the people you know together.

Make the most of yourself – for High-Affiliation people

A client of mine, Claudia, is the human resources director at a publishing company and she loves her job. She spends most of her time in meetings or coaching the members of her team. She loves the open-plan environment and recently argued against a motion to remodel the layout of the floor to give senior managers their own offices – she didn't want to be shut away from her team. She hates going through her emails or poring over the quarterly budgets – boring! When she speaks, she barely pauses for breath. I've rarely met anyone so full of bright-eyed enthusiasm and fun. Now forty-something, she is out socialising with friends – often people from work many years her junior – probably three or four nights a week. Oh, and she's the lead singer in a band in her spare time.

When I first coached her, she didn't think she could end up becoming the centre of attention. Only with some encouragement did she concede that her liveliness and energy could overwhelm a conversation. She admitted that she spent more time talking than listening. Often without realising it, she probably talked over other people.

High-Affiliation people can't help but shine brightly. Put you in a roomful of people and you're happy to talk and entertain. Claudia got the highest possible score on the Affiliation dimension. You're probably not as extreme, but might your challenges be similar?

Listen – no, *really* listen

> **"When people talk, listen completely. Most people never listen."**
>
> **Ernest Hemingway, author**

I remember taking home my first ever school report. I waited while my parents tore open the envelope and read my teachers' comments. The consistent theme was: 'Good work – would learn more by talking less.'

I get that you enjoy talking. You're a born raconteur, a storyteller. But if you're talking, you can't find out the other person's story, his or her personal interests and professional needs, dreams and aspirations, anything.

Or perhaps you listen, but only until you can jump in. I admit to hijacking a conversation occasionally. Someone will be talking and I'll be dying to make a point or tell an anecdote about a funny situation that happened to me.

But listening isn't simply about shutting your mouth. You probably know people who 'listen' while they're watching the TV, reading a newspaper, checking their BlackBerry. When they do that, they are effectively saying, 'You're not important enough for me to give you my full attention, so keep talking and I'll pick out the bits I find interesting.' I don't need to tell you not to be one of those types.

Even when we're giving someone eye contact, we're still not necessarily listening. It's also about stopping that internal, silent mental chatter, the voice in your head that allows you to wonder what to have for dinner even while you're nodding at the person in front of you.

You have a lot to say and you want to be helpful, funny, compassionate, empathetic. But without due care, you may occasionally blurt out your thoughts and cut people off before they've finished talking. You can take over before you've realised it. Not intentionally – it just happens.

It's even more likely to happen when you're in a position of power or authority. Researcher Ena Inesi at the London Business School tells me:

> *You have to understand where people come from to work together effectively. If you don't take their perspectives, you will be asking them for things that they are less motivated by or less able to do.*

So now's the time to cultivate that silent and mysterious air about you. Because people with gravitas wait until the other person has finished. They allow themselves the luxury of silence – a few moments to think about how to respond. They are happy to leave a pregnant pause in the air rather than blurt out their immediate thoughts.

It takes effort to listen with respect, to get across: 'I care enough about you as a person to give you my full attention.' To build strong relationships with the people who matter, you must *demonstrate* that you can listen intently. Can you do it?

Become your best: Focusing your attention with laser precision

How can you listen in a way that conveys to other people that they matter? Answer: all it takes is your willingness to do so.

Visualise that you have control of an imaginary spotlight. You can shine your spotlight on whatever you're focusing on, whatever you choose to pay attention to. You can focus on a task such as reading a newspaper, typing an email or staring out of the window over someone's shoulder. And like a spotlight, you can make it a very large circle to encompass several tasks at once, or a narrow beam to focus on one thing at a time. So you can read a book while being vaguely aware of the TV in the background. You can pay just enough attention to someone speaking during a meeting while you're writing a note to yourself on a completely unrelated topic. Or sit nodding as someone else is talking while you are miles away, thinking about the tasks you need to do.

When your spotlight has a very wide diameter, you're splitting your attention. You are doing both tasks, but neither of them very well. So make an effort to shrink the spotlight of your attention, to focus intently on one task at a time.

When you're with other people, be sure to narrow the spotlight of your attention and focus on them fully. Stop the other tasks. Lock your eyes on to the other person's eyes. Feel free to take notes on what other people are saying, but don't glance at your computer screen, the TV or out of the window. Don't let your thoughts roam. Concentrate only on what the other person is saying. Otherwise, you may as well get a T-shirt printed up that says:

- 'What you're saying isn't important enough, so I can read my emails at the same time.'

- '*You* are not important enough for me to give you the full weight of my attention.'
- 'What you're saying isn't very interesting so I'm doodling instead.'

Listening to what's *not* said

Listening is about more than simply paying attention and stopping whatever else you might want to be doing. That's step one, the easy bit. Step two is about reading between the lines.

Good listening is as much about understanding what's *not* being said as what is. Because people don't always say what they mean. A friend can say, 'I'm fine' while his voice trembles and he avoids looking at you. A colleague can say, 'It's not a big deal' about having just been promoted, even while she's fighting to hold back a grin.

When people speak, what are the *feelings* behind their words? Perhaps they're too shy to speak of their achievements and want you to praise them. Is it that their pride is under attack or they feel excited, insecure, unloved, angry, what?

Become your best: Summarising words *and* feelings

When it comes to important matters, High-Affiliation individuals can benefit from slowing down the pace of a conversation. That way, you avoid the risk of hijacking the discussion and taking over.

To demonstrate that you've been giving a person your utmost attention, challenge yourself to summarise the key points so far. Sometimes you may need to restate what's been said at length and other times in only a few words. Remember that what's *not* being said can carry more weight than the words that someone chooses to actually say.

If you're at all unsure about what a person is trying to express, you're always better off asking a question than making a statement. Saying, 'Would it be right to say that you're feeling upset?' is less presumptuous than, 'You're upset.'

Remember that this is not about you saying, 'It'll work out OK in the end' or 'Don't worry'. Neither should you try to jump in with your point of view or your advice. Not yet anyway. Summarising is purely about playing back to someone what you think has been said. Here are some examples of how to summarise:

- 'So Joanna snapped at you and you can't understand what you might have done.'
- 'Let me get this clear. You tried to reach Ian but he couldn't take your call. Derek's in a meeting. You have until 3 o'clock to sort it out and now you don't know what to do?'
- 'If I understand you correctly, you don't know whether to bring the matter up or hope that the problem will go away on its own?'
- 'You're really excited, aren't you?'

Sure, you may have a perfectly valid point you want to get across. But the first rule of dialogue is this: to get other people to listen to you, you must first listen to them. More than that, you have to *demonstrate* that you listened. Paraphrase, summarise, check that you understand. Once you have understood not only their words but also their feelings, you put yourself in a commanding position to state your case.

Decide when to speak – if at all

So now it's your turn to speak. Or is it?

Just because there's a pause in the conversation doesn't mean that it's time for you to speak up. Quieter Low-Affiliation people may need a few moments to compose their thoughts before speaking again. Get used to giving people those few moments.

Even when the pause in the conversation turns into a lengthy silence, you may still not need to speak. Because the key issue is whether or not you have something that's *worthwhile* enough to share.

I worked one on one with an executive who had been criticised during a recent performance review for being too hasty, for jumping to conclusions, for not listening. Working together, I helped him to conquer his instincts.

One day, he told me that he had made a breakthrough. He explained:

> *Before speaking, I take a moment to ask myself, 'Would my comment get a thumbs-up from someone?' If I can make a remark that genuinely moves the discussion on, I speak up. If what I want to say only show-cases how clever I am, I shut up.*

Another manager explained her tactic for becoming a better listener:

> *I still feel the desire to sort problems out for people and tell them what I'd do. But I've learned to hit the pause button and contribute by asking open-ended questions, such as, 'What can I do to help?' rather than telling others what I think they should do.*

Before you speak, hit the pause button and ask yourself: 'Am I going to get a thumbs-up?'

Turn your best intentions into action

The fact that you need to speak less and listen more probably isn't news. I'm guessing you realise you need to listen more.

Perhaps you've been told more than once that you broadcast more than you receive. Question is: Why don't you *do* it?

The reality is that you forget, have other matters on your mind. You get distracted. All of this is perfectly understandable, but it's not an excuse, a way to let yourself off the hook.

If it matters to you, you need to use reminders, colleagues and buddies to support you as you work on talking less and listening – *really* listening – more.

Here are some examples of how other people have done it:

- One client, Elizabeth, writes the word 'Listen' on the first blank page of her notebook before meetings.
- Another client, Mark, asked his personal assistant to rattle a jar every time he talks over her. Like a swear box, he puts £5 in each time he does it. To make it fun for his assistant, the proceeds don't go to charity – Mark tells her to spend the money on whatever she likes.
- Niall has asked his colleague and close friend Alistair to count the number of times he interrupts the conversation during meetings. Three times and Niall buys all the drinks on the next Friday evening.

Over to you

Your turn. How can you remind yourself to listen? How can you make it your new habit?

Give it some thought now. Asking people – friends or colleagues – to remind you is always handy. Making it a fun game for them can help. Including some twist of punishment may help you to pay attention every time you do it.

If you're serious about improving your listening skills, stop reading any further. Decide now on a way to make listening a new habit for you.

Give people space

You're a people-person, aren't you? Like most High-Affiliation individuals, you're probably energised by spending time with people.

When you're presented with an impasse or challenge, you'd like nothing better than to gather folks around you, talk it through and throw ideas around. When you have good news or a juicy piece of gossip, you want to share it straight away. Low-Affiliation people, however, prefer to reflect on problems and challenges on their own. They don't want their work interrupted by your news or gossip or even your help.

So here's a question for you. How many of the people around you are as people-loving and gregarious as you?

Consider the people you spend the most time with – your colleagues, your loved ones, your clients. Is your boss someone who might prefer to receive an update on your project by email rather than having you talk it through there and then? Is your other half someone who needs to recharge by watching TV in silence rather than talking about the day at work? Might any of the people in your life need a bit more time on their own – that is, away from you?

Become your best: Understanding what makes 'em tick

List the dozen (or more) people you interact with most frequently on a daily basis. This might include your colleagues, boss, close friends and people you live with.

Try to guess each person's position on the Affiliation continuum. Given how they behave, would you say that they are High-, Average- or Low-Affiliation people?

Low-Affiliation individuals often feel smothered by even moderate amounts of contact, discussion, spending time with others. If you guess that any of the people closest to you are in this category, how can you commit to giving them a little more space?

Be prepared to exile yourself. Leave others alone. Force yourself to shut your door or simply shut your mouth. Sit at your desk. Fight the urge to talk, share a joke and laugh together, gossip, ask what someone's up to. The quieter people in your life will thank you for it, honestly.

ONWARDS AND UPWARDS

Some of us tilt towards the more solitary end of the Affiliation spectrum, others towards the party-throwing end. Here's a quick summary of words and phrases to remind you of the key differences separating Low-Affiliation and High-Affiliation people.

Low Affiliation	**High Affiliation**
Tend to be a good listeners.	Tend to be good entertainers.
Prefer the company of familiar people.	Enjoy meeting new people.
Private about their thoughts and feelings.	Public about sharing thoughts and feelings.
Usually reserved, modest, quiet.	Typically gregarious, outgoing, loud.
Can work independently for long periods.	Can work with others for long periods.
Need to network more.	Need to listen more intently.

If you scored lower on Affiliation:

- Respect your nature. You are at your best when you can spend at least some time thinking, reflecting, working and being alone. As you consider options in work and life, steer clear of crowded environments and situations where you have to meet scores of new people every day.
- Remember that other people may need more face-to-face interaction than you. Commit to getting away from your desk, home, computer and phone – go and meet people, remind them what you have in common and cement your bonds with them.
- Appreciate that both your personal and professional life will be richer if you have a sturdy network of people to support, help and advise you. Think collaboration, cooperation, teamwork. Other people can help you to achieve more.
- Think of net*friending* rather than networking. You already have the skills to make more friends. Use your interests and pursuits to seek out like-minded people.

If you scored higher on Affiliation:

- Play to your strengths. You come alive when people surround you, allowing you to talk through ideas, discuss problems and jointly come up with solutions. So make sure you pursue opportunities in life that allow you to be with people. Projects involving solitary reflection, reading and research are not for you.
- Make a concerted effort to listen. Stop doing anything else, hold back your thoughts and opinions, and give the other person the full weight of your attention.
- Get used to paraphrasing what other people are saying and feeling. This is a great trick to check that you're not jumping to the wrong conclusions; you also demonstrate that you're listening intently.
- Recognise that not everyone else needs to spend as much time in company as you. Back off. Give people time on their own to think and recharge their batteries.

05

Conscientiousness

"The cautious seldom err."

Confucius

"What's the worst that could happen?"

Advertising slogan for Dr Pepper

Time to use your mind's eye. I want you to think about your favourite snack. What do you like to treat yourself with? Perhaps it's a bar of chocolate, a bacon sandwich, a tub of ice cream. A slab of cake, a portion of fish and chips, a bag of popcorn. Mmm … Whatever it is, I want you to imagine that you have it in front of you right now.

OK, now imagine that you have a short piece of work to do – it'll take you about 20 minutes to complete. You now have two choices. You can either enjoy your snack now and then start the work. Or finish the work first and reward yourself with the snack afterwards. Which would you choose?

That simple choice illustrates the two ends of the Conscientiousness spectrum. High-Conscientiousness people control their impulses. They are disciplined, organised and self-controlled. Low-Conscientiousness people happily follow their impulses and are spontaneous, fun-loving and adventurous.

There are advantages and disadvantages to both. High-Conscientiousness individuals are careful and hardly ever make mistakes, but can sometimes be too conservative, too risk-averse. Low-Conscientiousness individuals are adaptable and flexible, but can drive people crazy for being disorganised and taking too many risks.

Time to see how you measure up.

Your Conscientiousness

Questionnaire 4 on page 10 measures your Conscientiousness. Score two points each time you agreed with any of the following statements: 1, 3, 4, 7 and 9. Give yourself two points each time you disagreed with any of the statements: 2, 5, 6, 8 and 10. You should have a total score between 0 and 20.

A score of 8 or less suggests low levels of Conscientiousness. A score of 14 or more means that you have high levels of Conscientiousness. A score of 10 or 12 means that you have average levels of Conscientiousness.

Time to read the sections that are aimed at your personality profile. If you're average for Conscientiousness, you could probably do with being a bit more prudent, so focus on the advice within the Low-Conscientiousness sections. If you're high for Conscientiousness, learn to let go a little more.

What kind of person are you?

You can spot a child's level of Conscientiousness from as young as four years of age. Stanford University professor Walter Mischel brought four-year-olds into a room one by one and put a marshmallow on the table in front of them. He told the kids, 'You can eat this marshmallow right now if you like. But, if you can wait while I leave the room for a few minutes, you can have two marshmallows when I return.'

About a third of the kids ate the marshmallow straight away. Another third waited 20 minutes to receive two marshmallows. The remaining third of the children waited for a little while, but ultimately gave up and succumbed to the temptation of the single marshmallow in front of them.

The Low-Conscientiousness person: the swashbuckling opportunist

As a kid, you would have been one of those who ate the marshmallow pretty quickly because you're someone who lives for the here and now.

You're a flexible, adaptable person who enjoys dynamic, changing situations. Others may prefer the routine of a conventional 9 to 5 existence, of having a job that is the same day in, day out. But that would bore you stupid. While others hate uncertainty, you thrive on living in the moment, not knowing what might happen from one day to the next.

In your personal life too, you dislike being tied down by plans. Others may want to schedule ahead for weeks and months in advance, but you don't want to have every evening and weekend mapped out for the foreseeable future. Whatever happened to spontaneity?

You may get infuriated by 'paralysis analysis', by people who sit on the sidelines endlessly debating the right thing to do. If you spot an opportunity, you'd rather give it a go and see what comes off. *Carpe diem*. Seize the day. If you had to pick a modern-day slogan, perhaps you'd choose Nike's 'Just Do It'. Clichés, of course, but you feel that life is too short to watch it pass by.

And if something goes wrong, you're adaptable. You'll survive. You'll respond to the needs of the moment. You'll change tactics and try it another way. Better to learn from what you did than regret what you didn't do.

You find rules and red tape tedious. You feel that the ends justify the means. So rather than follow overly restrictive rules that stop you from achieving your goals, you're happy to bend them.

And don't get you started on filling in forms and doing paper-work. You understand that some of the books need keeping. But in an ideal world, you'd do away with all of that needless, yawn-some bureaucracy.

You're happy to take risks. You embrace change. You think on your feet. All qualities that serve you well in a furiously paced and ever-changing world.

The High-Conscientiousness person: the good organisational citizen

As a child, you would have been happy to wait to get that second marshmallow. Because you're patient and the kind of person who thinks before acting.

You're a trustworthy, dependable, organised person. Others may be impetuous, erratic or forgetful, but not you. Friends rely on your incredible ability to get things done – to keep track of important dates, pick up tickets, make dinner reservations, find the best deals. Colleagues envy your ability to keep on top of everything. You always deliver; you're a safe pair of hands.

You set high standards for yourself and others. You have a good level of attention to detail and you make few mistakes. That's because you take the time to gather the facts, weigh up the pros and cons, and make a reasoned decision. Fools rush in, don't they?

The world is full of traps and pitfalls that can befall the unwary – anything from forgetting to pack your passport before leaving for the airport to leaving a report until the last minute. But those kinds of things don't happen to you. You identify what needs doing. You make lists, weigh up options and leave little to chance.

In fact, your natural instinct is to impose order on your environment. You may not necessarily be neat and tidy, but you prefer to reduce unpredictability by making plans. You control, manage and orchestrate the world around you. If something could go wrong, you'd rather have considered the contingency and be ready for it than simply hope it won't happen. Better safe than sorry.

You respect the rules of the game too. Rules are there for a reason. Whether in your work life or your home life, you like to know what is acceptable and what is out of bounds.

You're careful. You can be trusted. You never let people down. All qualities that make you a loyal friend and exemplary organisational citizen.

Make the most of yourself – for Low-Conscientiousness people

Let's get one thing straight. You will never be great at dotting the 'i's and crossing the 't's. Following strict rules and guidelines, focusing constantly on detail, and repeating routines over and over again taps into all of your weak spots. So why do it?

Play to your strengths, not your weaknesses

You will do well in entrepreneurial settings and creative jobs where breaking the rules, challenging the status quo and even shocking people occasionally are considered positive outcomes.

Avoid large organisations with time-honoured traditions where the way of doing things is, has been and always will be the same. To thrive, you must find environments in which you can capitalise on your strong points.

That's not to say that you can get away with flouting *every* rule. There are some rules that must be obeyed if you don't want to crash and burn. Perhaps for reasons of health and safety – to avoid lives or limbs being in jeopardy. Or so you don't risk big fines from a regulator. The bosses at Enron, the US business that combusted so spectacularly back in 2001, provide a great example of what can happen when Low-Conscientiousness people are so focused on achieving their goals that they forget which rules mustn't be broken. If, however, you understand the rules that absolutely, positively, 100 per cent of the time must be adhered to, you can then proceed to break the rest with impunity.

So think about your current job. How much of your time do you spend having to follow rules and regulations, policies and procedures? Now ask yourself, 'Am I happy doing that for the rest of my life?

Over to you

Here are some questions to stimulate your thinking. What kind of work might be better suited to your adaptable, opportunistic nature?

- Without quitting your job, how could you pursue more projects that play to your strengths? Consider projects that allow you to focus on strategy and the big picture rather than the detail of implementation. Or work that encourages you to change your approach to meet the needs of different colleagues or customers rather than delivering the same script every time. Go to your boss, explain the kind of work you'd most enjoy (and perform best at) and see if you can change the direction of your career.
- Which of your friends or colleagues do you envy for the amount of freedom that they have in their work? Go talk to them. See what you can learn. And if you love what you hear, explore how you could switch careers.
- What hobbies or pursuits might allow you to express your irrepressible nature outside of work? If you *have* to be rigorous and careful at work, at least look for something outside of work that allows you to be yourself.

Get organised

Being spontaneous has its upside – you respond quickly to opportunities, while others are still mulling over what is the best course of action. But your aversion to detailed planning and reluctance to be tied down mean that other people may see you as disorganised.

So you need to fight your inner rebel. Get more organised, even though it's not your ideal way of working. Otherwise no boss is going to recommend you for a promotion if it looks like you're struggling to stay on top of the work you have now. No client will let you make the same mistake twice. Even loved ones may feel let down when you forget birthdays or important events. Sure, *you* may feel that you're coping just fine. But everyone else who is higher on Conscientiousness than you – and that's most people – will notice when you forget appointments, make mistakes and lose track of anything from a piece of paperwork to entire projects.

Look at it another way. Say you go to a restaurant with a large group of friends. When a waiter takes your table's order and doesn't write anything down, doesn't that make you nervous? You feel so much better when the waiter writes it all down. Even better when he repeats it back to you, emphasising that the sirloin should be medium-rare and the T-bone well done, plus no dressing on the side salad.

Or imagine if an architect came to your home to discuss putting in a spanking new kitchen, knocking down walls and changing the entire layout of your living space. He measures up the rooms and says that he'll commit them to memory. Hold on. *Memory*? Wouldn't you feel a little more secure if he wrote it all down? And preferably not on a ragged scrap of paper, but in a notebook or some kind of folder.

Become your best: Relying on systems and people

When it comes to making a great impact on the people you know, it's not so much how organised you are as how organised they *perceive* you to be. History probably tells them that you're not that disciplined.

Time to turn over a new leaf. Get a system that works for you. Scribbling notes on separate pieces of paper or Post-it notes is not very effective.

Use a diary, an electronic organiser, a wall chart, whatever works for you. Writing things down in front of your colleagues, your boss, your loved ones can have a rather mesmerising effect on them. The simple act of writing it down helps them to believe that it might actually get done.

Look among your friends and colleagues for people who are completely on top of their work. Ask them how they do it. Learn from them. Adopt their system or adapt it to make it work for you.

I realise that this may be painful advice for you. You hate to feel shackled by lists and plans and all this attention to detail sounds like such a drag. But I'm not suggesting that you have to be anywhere near as meticulous or, frankly, uptight as some of your High-Conscientiousness counterparts – just a little more organised than you would naturally like to be. This is ultimately about winning other people's trust that you won't let them down.

If you're lucky, you may be in a position to hire someone to pick up the pieces after you. Perhaps an accountant to keep track of your finances. A personal assistant to book in appointments and make sure that you turn up on time. Or a deputy manager or chief of staff whose sole purpose is to make sure nothing falls through the cracks.

If you have the money to do it, I strongly suggest surrounding yourself with the best people money can buy. And by 'best', I mean people who are diligent, careful and good when it comes to attention to detail. Certainly, this is a must if you work for yourself. I work with so many entrepreneurs and senior managers who tell me that their personal assistants or seconds-in-command are worth their weight in gold.

I coach Rebecca Harper, who runs recruitment agency Grade A. She's fun to be around, but – like many Low-Conscientiousness people – boy did she used to be forgetful. I surveyed her clients and they'd been frustrated by her absent-mindedness more than a few times. Her solution? She bought a beautiful, leather-bound notebook. Now when she says that she's going to send me a book or set up a meeting to introduce me to someone, she writes it in her ever-present notebook, and I *know* it's going to happen. So people *can* change. Keep up the good work, Rebecca!

Impose structure on others and they will thank you for it

Say you invite a friend to join you for dinner one evening. You explain that you'll cook the main course if she will make a dessert. When she asks, 'What time should I come round and what should I make?' you reply, 'I'll be in all evening so come whenever suits you and bring whatever you like.'

That may seem perfectly accommodating on your part, but you must learn that for many people, too much freedom of choice isn't a good thing. They see it as uncertainty, a lack of clarity, something to fret over. If your friend is of the High-Conscientiousness persuasion, she may worry over exactly what time to arrive. Would 7 o'clock be too early? What if you're still doing something else and she interrupts you? Would 8 o'clock mean that you would end up eating too late though? And what should she bring for dessert? Without knowing what you intend to cook, she may worry that her contribution will clash with your meal rather than complement it.

As a Low-Conscientiousness person, you probably think this scenario is ridiculous. How could someone get worked up over something so *trivial*? What you must, must realise is that other people are wired in differently. Seriously, you must. Because where you see freedom to choose how to behave, others may see a lack of clarity. When you feel a sense of autonomy, others may feel uncertainty over what they're supposed to do or how they're supposed to do it. They can feel like they've been dumped into the middle of a situation, that they're being given insufficient guidance, support or leadership to perform at their best. And in the ensuing confusion, you could easily end up with disappointment.

Of course, a little mix-up between friends over dinner is hardly disastrous. But you may come to more grief if you're giving instructions to a decorator over which areas of your house you want repainting and which ones absolutely must not be touched. Or if you're telling a colleague or a supplier what you expect out of the major new project you're embarking on together.

So consider how you give instructions. You may enjoy having a wide remit, but others may see it as being cast adrift. Be prepared to give more guidance to others than you need for yourself. You need to let people know what you expect of them.

Become your best: Giving clear instructions

Always bear in mind that while you see too much direction as stifling and unnecessary, other people may appreciate that guidance and clarity. When briefing people, use the following questions as a checklist and make sure that you can tick off everything that others may wish to know:

- **What do you expect of a successful conclusion?** What are the final results, the products, the outcomes that you want? If you give vague instructions, such as, 'Please produce a great brochure to launch the new product', would you be as happy with a two-page leaflet instead of a full-blown catalogue or one in black and white versus full colour? Often, giving clear instructions is as much about saying what's off limits as what you want to see.
- **How do you expect it to be done?** What is the approach, the process, the method you recommend? What are the tools or resources you suggest for the task? How much money is available? You may not wish to be too prescriptive, but remember that others will probably

appreciate a little advice on how to tackle the task. Explain that you are giving suggestions as to how it could be done, but you would welcome an alternative approach too. That way you give guidance, but also provide the option to do it differently (and hopefully better).

- **When do you expect it to be done?** What's the deadline for the overall task or project? Again, be careful of fuzzy language. Does 'by the end of the year' mean by 31 December or the end of the financial year, in the spring? Consider if it would make sense to have mini-deadlines along the way to measure progress and check that the work is on track. If the overall deadline isn't for several months, you would be wise to check how people are getting on perhaps monthly or every few weeks, for example. Better to catch problems and crossed wires early on than discover at the very end that things have gone horribly, terribly wrong.
- **Why is this task important?** People often perform much better when they have at least some appreciation of the context for the task. If you can explain how people's work fits into the bigger picture, you help your High-Conscientiousness counterparts to avoid getting too bogged down in detail. Consider also which aspects or components of the task are most important. If you ask someone to do A, B and C, are they equally important? Or are any parts of the task more critical than others?

Slow down to contemplate, deliberate, plan

I worked one on one with Michael, a Low-Conscientiousness company director, who told me:

> *I deal with all of my emails as they come in. I read an email and respond to it straight away, but occasionally I realise the moment I've hit the send button that the email was too blunt or half complete and that I should have mentioned another couple of points.*

I shared with Michael a tip I'd read somewhere: that you can save emails as drafts rather than send them right away. Now he replies to emails as they come in, but only hits the send button three or four times a day, say at 10 a.m., lunchtime, 2 p.m. and 5 p.m. That gives him a couple of hours after composing an email to go back and change something if he needs to, which he does frequently.

But what was more interesting was how Michael made decisions in all quarters of his life. He once took a job and quit three weeks later. He had proposed to his first wife within two months of meeting her. And he had – a long time ago – stolen a bar stool from a pub as a dare at university. He admitted that he often saw decisions as challenges taunting and goading him into action.

You probably make lightning decisions in at least some areas of your life. Perhaps you're considering something as relatively mundane as how to respond to an email or what bottle of wine to pick up at the supermarket. Maybe it's a bit more important, such as deciding whether to quit a relationship or start a new job. In any case, you don't see the point of pondering it for too long – you hanker for action.

But moving too quickly could occasionally be rash or downright crazy.

High achievers – such as leading entrepreneurs and philanthropists – often make it *seem* as if they have charged ahead, that they are the first to launch the world's first this or that. But what we see is often the stage-managed press launch of initiatives that may have been months or even years in the making. Successful people are never reckless. They weigh up pros and cons and decide on the level of risk they're willing to take.

I recently met Patrick White, serial entrepreneur and former chief executive of several large international businesses. His last business had 600 staff and made US$2 billion a year. Now a multimillionaire with properties around the world, he shared with me the secret of his success. He called it his 'six Ps': 'Prior planning prevents piss-poor performance'. Sage words.

Become your best: Making truly great decisions

Real emergencies are rare. Few decisions have to be made in a matter of moments. So before you throw your energies behind any project, ask yourself these questions:

- Why are you pursuing this right now?
- What are the pros and cons of waiting 24 hours, a week, a month?
- How long would it take to become better prepared? Is that too long?
- Who should you ideally have onside to make this a success? And who (if anyone) do you already have onside?
- Do you have the expertise, resources, experience and credibility to make this work?

Just 10 to 15 minutes. That's all I'm suggesting. Take a quarter of an hour to work through these five questions and you will help yourself to gauge whether your idea is sure to be a winner.

I'm not recommending that you take the painstaking and sluggish approach to decision making that certain High-Conscientiousness people may advocate. Slowing down, though, even a little – at least with the bigger decisions in life – can pay huge dividends.

Anna Gillespie, a newly recruited marketing director, admitted that her eagerness led her to make many snap decisions.

> *I took on a great team with lots of ideas and I love to respond to them. If it's new, I always see the upside and want to give it a go. Six months into the job, the managing director took me aside and said that our marketing didn't have a focus. In trying to do everything, I was achieving nothing. Plus, what I didn't realise was that every time I*

switched direction, I was confusing and exhausting my team. The moment they got good at something, I'd change the rules of the game.

Her solution?

Whenever I hear a new suggestion, I say, 'Let me think about it.' It is so simple, but forcing myself to take 24 hours to ponder an idea is usually enough to make a more reasoned decision.

Slow down. Fight your gut instinct. Ask yourself a handful of questions and you ensure you make decisions that are considered risks rather than reckless ones.

Make the most of yourself – for High-Conscientiousness people

You're the go-to guy or gal for getting things done. If a friend needs someone to organise a surprise birthday party, you're the one who can be relied upon to find a venue, book a caterer, send out the invitations and make sure everything is perfect when the guest of honour walks through the door. If your boss needs someone to oversee a complex project, you can work out who should be doing what and by when, and how much it will cost.

The tendency to think ahead makes High-Conscientiousness people a real asset to most organisations as well as to themselves. Health researchers Margaret Kern and Howard Friedman even noticed that High-Conscientiousness people tend to live between two to four years longer than low scorers, possibly because they are more careful about their health as well as everything else.

As a High-Conscientiousness person, you do what's right, playing by the rules and delivering results. But your attention to detail, high standards and enthusiasm for plans can be as much of a weakness as a strength.

Go with the floe

No, that's not a typo. Dr John Nicholson, a leading psychologist in the 80s and 90s and an ex-boss of mine, likened life to skating on ice floes – the sheets of floating ice that sometimes detach themselves from the vast ice fields blanketing the Earth's poles. If you're on one of those drifting slabs of ice, you can never predict where the currents will push you.

And that's a pretty good metaphor for life. No matter how hard you may try to control your circumstances, you will always be affected by unpredictable currents. In fact, change is the only constant. Technology moves at dizzying speeds. Fashions and tastes move on. Governments come and go. Countries go to war and new countries are born. Businesses grow and shrink, perhaps adding new people to the team, firing them or changing everyone's roles. Friends move away and new friends come into our lives. All around us, people are born, people die and everyone in between gets older.

So my point is this: no plan can take into account everything that could possibly happen. No venture in life can be 100 per cent certain. Life is inherently messy, unpredictable and fraught with ambiguity. Whether you're trying to find The One, your perfect partner in life, or launching a multi-million pound project, you have to accept that there will always be an element of chance involved. The key to life isn't about holding back, it's about taking action despite what could go wrong.

Do it anyway

A smart buddy of mine often says, 'In the short term, we regret the things we did, but, over time, we regret the things we *didn't* do.' And he's right.

High-Conscientiousness people are sometimes slow to act. Perhaps you're like this too – wanting to be certain that your decisions will turn out right.

Sure, you could stay in the same job because you know it feels safe. You could decide that's better than trying your hand at something more exciting – perhaps a new job or setting up your own business. But then you could decide never to holiday abroad to avoid all those diseases, the humidity, the strange food, the risk of terrorism.

Isn't it better to give something a go and say that you tried than get to the end of your life and say that you played it safe? Do you want to be a quitter because you quit before you even started?

No, of course not.

Over to you

As a High-Conscientiousness person, you're probably more cautious in your decision making than many other people. But do you always need to be quite so careful in your approach?

Reflect for a moment and consider a decision that you regret *not* having made.

- What was the situation?
- What did you fear would happen?
- What actually happened?
- What would you do differently?

We all have to make decisions about the future. Sadly, we don't have the benefit of a crystal ball to guarantee our success. We must all accept that there's an element of risk with most decisions.

High achievers are willing – at least occasionally – to make bold moves, to take intelligent gambles. That's not to say they're happy taking brazen or ludicrous risks. Instead, they accept that no venture can be entirely without risk. They weigh up the pros and cons and plan for the worst eventuality, but hope for the best. And you can too.

Become your best: Making decisions that lead to action

Should you take that new job or promotion? Should you embark on a new project or decide to start a family? Questions, questions, questions.

You will never have enough information to make the perfect decision. Life is about making decisions based on the information you do have. Bear in mind that deciding *not* to move forwards is making a decision to stick with the status quo, to put up with the circumstances you're currently in.

Here's a step-by-step technique for making those big decisions and moving forward regardless:

1 **Define the situation, problem or opportunity.** Write a few lines about it. Seeing your thoughts on paper can help you to consider them more rationally than if you simply allow the thoughts to bounce around your head.

2 **List your options.** Try to come up with *at least* four different options. Avoid getting into black-and-white thinking that allows for either one choice or another. Look for shades of grey that permit you to act but without risking everything at once. If you're thinking of quitting your job for a new one, perhaps you can negotiate to spend a few days shadowing your prospective boss or meeting members of the team one on one rather than accepting it straight away. If you're thinking of leaving your partner, consider a trial separation as an option or moving in with a friend for a week first. Seeking at least four different options may point up alternatives, allowing you to move forwards without committing everything at once.

3 **Complete a table for each option.** In terms of consequences, think not only about yourself but also those who are close to you – perhaps your family or a business partner. Include in your assessment factors such as how your values, finances, health and happiness may be

affected. Use your judgement to decide what counts as short- versus medium- and long-term consequences. The long-term consequences of, for example, taking out a huge loan to start up a business may be more far-reaching than the consequences of taking an assignment in another part of the country for the company you currently work for. Don't worry too much about the timeframes – focus simply on listing the pros and cons for your different options.

	Short term	**Medium term**	**Long term**
Positive consequences			
Negative consequences			

4 **Identify the rational best option.** If you were advising a friend on this issue, which option would you recommend that he or she take? That's not necessarily the right option for you though. You still have one concluding step to take.

5 **How do you *feel* about each option?** Gut instinct is much maligned by rational decision makers, but facts don't always give us the right answers. In fact, the first four steps of this process are not designed to give you the answer; they are designed to tap into your feelings and intuition. If you have a sense of trepidation about one option, but feel a hit of excitement when you consider another, that may be all you need to make a decision that's right for you.

Yes, there can be a time and place for gathering data and research. But all successful people eventually have to rely on their instincts. Ted Turner, founder of 24-hour news channel CNN, wrote in his autobiography:

> *Henry Ford didn't need focus groups to tell him that people would prefer inexpensive, dependable automobiles over horses, and I doubt that Alexander Graham Bell stopped to worry about whether people would prefer speaking to each other on the phone.*

So when he started his news channel, he didn't conduct any formal research about it either. He thought about it, weighed up the likely consequences, then did it.

Your feelings are part of what makes you human. Psychologist and author Marsha Linehan says that people who make decisions based purely on facts and logic are trapped in a state of 'reasonable mind'. On the other hand, people who make decisions based too heavily on their emotions are caught up in 'emotion mind'. Only people who integrate thoughts and instincts, facts with feelings, can experience the balance of 'wise mind'.

Learn to trust your judgement. Don't be too calculating in all you do. You may be surprised how good your decisions can be.

Break the rules – at least occasionally

High-Conscientiousness individuals are usually loyal friends, stalwart team players and great organisational citizens because they find it easy to play within the rules of the game. If an organisation says that all decisions can only be made by managers at Grade 7 and above, you probably know better than to break the rules. If your spouse says that you should put the kids to bed at 9 o'clock, you will make every effort to do so.

But high achievers rarely play entirely by the rules.

Because rules can outlive their usefulness, over time they can get in the way of progress. Take the rule that you should put the kids to bed at 9 o'clock. Sure, that's fine when you have an eight-year-old. But at some point, as they reach 10 or 11, 12 or 13 or older, you have to let your kids stay up a little later. You can't keep sending them off to bed at 9 o'clock when they're 22!

Same goes for the workplace. Say there's a rule stopping you and other employees at your grade from making decisions involving more than £10,000. Anything over that and you have to submit a formal proposal and await sign-off from your boss. It makes sense initially, when you're new to the job. But then you get better at the job. You gain experience. You know the job inside out – certainly better than the fresh-faced manager who's just been parachuted in as your new boss.

Imagine now that your new boss isn't coping with the workload. The proposals are piling up in his in-tray, customers are fuming and nothing is getting done. You could wait for him to drown under paperwork and customers to walk away because the rule says that you have to leave the big decisions to him. But you know the job, so you could place the orders yourself. Technically, that's breaking the rules; but it would get the work done, keep customers happy and get your new boss out of a jam.

Many organisations have bureaucratic rules that seem to stop people from succeeding rather than helping them. Many rules are merely habits or routines that people have done for ages and got used to.

'That's the way it is.'

'That's just how we do it.'

But rather than adhering rigidly to the rulebook, ask yourself, 'Why? What's the intention behind the rule? Is it still fit for purpose?'

'It always helps to have someone who can say, "No, we can do it faster this way" or "We have to break the rules, even our own rules, to get things done",' argues Tom Anderson, mega-multi-millionaire co-founder of social networking site MySpace. Tradition said that people maintained friendships in person or over the phone. But websites such as MySpace and Facebook challenged those old conventions, creating a multi-billion dollar sector in the process.

Rules need to be constantly reviewed to establish if they are still appropriate. You may need to challenge conventional thinking, make people uncomfortable and push the boundaries of what's accepted. Are you ready to be – at least occasionally – the non-conformist, the rule-breaker, the one to shake things up?

Become your best: Challenging your own set of conventions

Rules and regulations can act as useful guidelines for our behaviour. You wouldn't want an airline pilot to deviate from established safety protocols when landing the plane you're on, would you? And what about a heart surgeon trying out a crazy new idea she overheard when your loved one is on the operating table? That said, yesterday's rules can quickly turn into shackles if we obey them mindlessly. The world moves on and what may have worked in the past could stop us from being effective or more creative in the future.

This exercise is aimed at periodically shaking up the rules, assumptions and values that you follow. Simply complete the following sentences:

- People would be upset if I . . .
- It would be wrong to . . .

Two simple sentences, but so many ways you could complete them. And that's the test here. Aim to use the two sentences to come up with *at least* 100 complete sentences. That may sound like quite a lot, but the first couple of dozen sentences you come up with won't really challenge your assumptions. You only discover your unspoken assumptions when you push yourself to the limits. I suggest that you do this exercise perhaps once or twice a year.

You can do this either on your own, to scrutinise your own life, or with a team at work, to examine the rules that bind your organisation. The idea is to consider all of the rules, conventions, assumptions and established ways of doing things. Once you've listed them, consider why people would be upset or why it would be wrong. Would *everyone* be upset? Would it be wrong in *every* situation? Do or would any of your friends, customers or rivals do it differently?

Let's see how this challenging might work in practice.

In your personal life, you might say, 'People would be upset if I quit my job.' But *who* would be upset? Which is more important to you – your own job satisfaction and mental health or the expectations that your friends and relatives may have of you?

More controversially, you might think, 'It would be wrong for my teenage daughter to have sex until she is married.' But consider the pros and cons of your rule. Sure, you might be able to persuade her not to have sex. Alternatively, she could end up having sex anyway, but feel unable to tell you about it because you made the topic taboo. Would a more flexible rule be more appropriate?

At work, say a colleague comes up with the sentence: 'It would be wrong to give away our product for free.' Well, would it? Other businesses do that. They allow customers to use a product online and benefit from advertising to make a few pennies every time a customer accesses the web page. They offer freebies, knowing that customers often feel obligated to make some other purchase. Alternatively, a business could offer the product for free for the first three months, hoping in that time to persuade customers the product is so good they can't live without it.

Accepting the established rules is allowing yourself to stagnate. Challenge the rules you hold dear – at least once in a while.

Let go of the small stuff

You have high standards. And let's be honest, you probably produce work that is of higher quality than many of the people around you. You work harder, you pay more attention, you care more – which is great when you have the time to work at your own pace.

But what happens when you're under time pressure, when you have more work than hours in the day? If you have multiple tasks but know that you can only carry out a handful of them. How do you cope?

Suppose you have to get a proposal to a prospective client. The deadline is 5 o'clock on Friday afternoon. The client has repeatedly stated that late submissions won't be considered – they won't even be read. Your boss has only just asked you to work on it, so you have less than three hours to write an entire proposal that has always taken you at least six hours to complete. What would you do?

I coach quite a few High-Conscientiousness people who struggle with their workloads. They care so much about their work and hate to see a document go out with even a single typo or misaligned paragraph. But when there's too much to do, you need to prioritise. Sometimes it's better to produce something that is 'good enough' rather than let down a client, teacher, friend or colleague.

I worked with Anoushka, a High-Conscientiousness executive who took a new job to build a new division within an engineering firm. Three weeks in and she was hating it. She hadn't had the time to pull together a plan because she spent all of her time in meetings. She had 20 to 30 meetings every week, often overlapping, taking up 30 to 40 hours of her week. Colleagues were all so keen to make her feel included and she was afraid to say no because she didn't want to appear standoffish.

I helped her to see that most of the meetings weren't helping her to achieve her goals. Within the year, she would be judged on the quality of the team she brought on board and the money they made, not on the number of meetings she attended. So we worked together on prioritising. On pruning her schedule, saying no to a few meetings and freeing time up to work on the plan for her new division.

For other meetings, she decided that she would simply walk out, explaining to colleagues that she could only stay for part of the meeting and then leave when she'd got the gist. Yes, some people initially thought it was a little rude, but she created space in her diary to formulate her business plan, recruit a team, and seek out and win new customers. Ultimately, the money she brought in for the firm proved that she had taken the right approach.

Learn to prioritise. Scrutinise your schedule and ruthlessly focus on what you absolutely must do. Only then can you be truly effective.

Become your best: Applying the 80/20 rule

What do property, pea harvests and an Italian economist have to do with your effectiveness?

Quite a lot actually. In the nineteenth century, Italian economist Vilfredo Pareto identified that 80 per cent of property in Italy was owned by only 20 per cent of its people. He also spotted that 80 per cent of the pea harvest in his garden came from 20 per cent of his peapods. From this we get the famous Pareto principle, the 80/20 rule, which states that 80 per cent of the output you get comes from only 20 per cent of your inputs.

It's probably true of how you spend your time too. Of the tasks you need to do during your day, only a proportion of them *really* matter. Let's not argue whether it's a little more or less than 20 per cent of your tasks. The point is that a small proportion are more important than others.

Say you're packing your suitcase to go on holiday or a business trip at short notice. Sure, you would *like* to take pressed shirts with you and think carefully about what to pack for when you get there. But some tasks are more important than others – like making sure that you've got your tickets and passport and whatever work you may need for your trip. Those are the 20 per cent that count.

Say you need to write a report for your client. You would be better off spending your time putting together some bullet points with the key information you need to convey than making sure it's all formatted beautifully. Better to get the bare bones of your pitch across than not to hand it in at all.

We're all inundated by demands on our time but, when we have too much to do, we should separate what is important from what is merely urgent. We need to focus on what we *must* do – what will deliver the greatest benefit – as opposed to what may be clamouring most loudly for our attention.

Do you already make lists of tasks you need to achieve each day? If you don't, then making one is a good start. Draw up a list at the end of every day of all the tasks that you need to do the next day. Then note down the most critical ones. Of course, many of your tasks are important, but some are genuinely critical. Those are the ones that will make the biggest difference to your day, your career, your life. So which are they? Which are the ones that you should underline, put a star against, mark up with a highlighter – at least in your head if not actually on paper?

Prioritise how you will spend your time the next day. Get used to taking that perspective on all of your work and tasks in life too. Keep reprioritising throughout the day. When you are handed a new task to do, consider whether it is a 'must do' or merely a 'should do, if I have time'. If you believe that a new task is critical and must be done, then one other 'must do' task has to fall off the list.

Don't step into the trap of trying to squeeze more and more work into your day. The whole point of prioritising is to ensure that you complete the few tasks that add the most value, the roughly 20 per cent that make 80 per cent of the difference.

Play to your strengths

The advice in this section shows you how you need to adjust to shifting priorities and be more adaptable some of the time. However, I'm not suggesting you should aim to become the kind of disruptive risk-taker that Low-Conscientiousness individuals can be.

In fact, you will thrive and feel most fulfilled when you can play to your strong points, when you can make plans, organise your world, and be careful and considered with your decisions. So bear that in mind as you pursue future opportunities. If you're looking for a new job, look to join a team or pick a role that respects planning and forethought. Perhaps you may be best off in a large organisation with established traditions and conventions. Avoid situations that require seat-of-the-pants decision making in chaotic and ever-changing environments.

In your personal life, recognise that you will always be frustrated by Low-Conscientiousness people who hate being tied down by plans. But also realise that you will never change them. You can either put up with them or move away from having them in your life.

Respect your preferences and strengths. Then you can be both successful *and* fulfilled.

ONWARDS AND UPWARDS

Remember that Conscientiousness – like each of the other personality dimensions – is a continuum. Even two people who are both Low-Conscientiousness may behave in different ways from each other if one is actually much lower than the other. Same goes for two High-Conscientiousness individuals.

Neither end of the range is innately better than the other. When I work with teams, I notice that bosses often recruit people who are all like themselves – leading to entire teams consisting of rule-breaking mavericks who throw themselves into massively risky situations or overly careful planners who analyse everything to the nth degree. The lesson? You need a bit of both. If you're a Low-Conscientiousness individual, get more organised and structured for the sake of yourself *and* those around you. If you're a High-Conscientiousness person, learn to let go a little more, to take the occasional gamble.

Here's a rough and ready reminder of the key differences between the two ends of the spectrum:

Low-Conscientiousness	**High-Conscientiousness**
Enjoy challenging the status quo.	Behave as good organisational citizens.
Typically adaptable, spontaneous, unorthodox.	Tend to be organised, careful, prudent.
Jump in.	Hold back.
May take on too many risks.	May be too risk-averse.
Break rules and push boundaries.	Adhere to rules and live within boundaries.
May be seen as disorganised, unreliable.	May be seen as uptight, inflexible.

If you scored lower for Conscientiousness:

- Look for unstructured, entrepreneurial environments and steer clear of environments that require lots of rules and bureaucracy. That way you can be yourself and play to your strengths.
- Get at least a little bit more organised and take slightly more time over your decisions. Otherwise, people may see you as disorganised and unreliable – and those kinds of perceptions

may make them reluctant to trust you with more responsibility or promotions.

- When giving instructions or delegating work, be sure to give others more guidance than you need for yourself. Remember that, while you may not enjoy being told what to do, others will probably appreciate the extra support.

If you have a somewhat higher score for Conscientiousness:

- Bear in mind that most situations in life require us to make decisions without having all of the information we need. No decision can ever be guaranteed. All you can do is plan for any eventuality and then do it anyway.
- Occasionally question the rules and assumptions that you feel obliged to follow. Consider at least once a year which of the rules – in both your personal and professional life – may need review.
- Recognise that your high standards can be both a strength and a weakness. When you have too much work, remember that 'good enough' is sometimes more appropriate than perfect. Use the Pareto principle, the 80/20 rule, to prioritise and focus on what's most important.

06

Sensitivity

"The great gift of human beings is that we have the power of empathy."
Meryl Streep, actress

It's Saturday night and you've arranged to go out for dinner with a friend. Your friend asks, 'Where would you like to go for dinner?' Are you the kind of person who answers the question with a question, replying, 'I don't mind – what would you like for dinner?' Or do you speak your mind, perhaps saying that you'd quite like to try the new French restaurant or have a serious craving for Thai food?

Sensitivity is the personality dimension that describes the extent to which you put the needs of other people above those of yourself. People who score highly on Sensitivity are incredibly attuned, sensitive to others' feelings. They put other people's needs ahead of their own. By replying that you don't mind where you go for dinner, you may end up eating at an Indian restaurant, even though Indian may secretly be your least favourite kind of food.

Lydia, a friend of mine, is so high on the Sensitivity scale that she always puts everyone else first. Whether someone's talking to her about what film to go and see, where to go for dinner, what projects to give her at work, how she'd like to decorate her home, she rarely expresses an opinion because she's so content to be a good friend, a good colleague, a good wife.

People who are low on Sensitivity are much more direct and to the point. They say what they think. Take Simon Cowell, for example. The famously forthright judge on shows such as *Britain's Got Talent* and *The X Factor* earns $40 million a year for appearing on *American Idol* alone. And what does he do? He speaks his mind. He tells performing artists what he thinks. Most people are too afraid to say to someone's face, 'You're rubbish', but not Simon. He simply says what the viewers at home are probably thinking anyway. I can't imagine that Simon would ask what you would want for dinner in our scenario above. He'd simply tell you what he wanted to do.

Lydia and Simon inhabit the two far ends of the Sensitivity spectrum. How do you stack up?

Your Sensitivity

Flick back to Questionnaire 5 on page 12. Award yourself two points each time you agreed with any of the following statements: 2, 4, 6 and 8. Award yourself two points every time you disagreed with any of the statements numbered 1, 3, 5, 7, 9 and 10. You should have a score between 0 and 20.

A score of 10 or less suggests you're low on Sensitivity. A score of 16 or more suggests that you're high on Sensitivity. A score between 12 and 14 suggests that you have fairly average levels of Sensitivity.

Find the sections in the rest of this chapter that relate to your personality profile. If you're average for Sensitivity, you may need to read both descriptions and pick the advice that seems best suited to you.

What kind of person are you?

As with each personality dimension, your level of Sensitivity affords you a unique set of talents. Low-Sensitivity people are good at making tough decisions, while High-Sensitivity people are more tender-minded, caring individuals who naturally seek to please others. Whether you're tough or tender – or somewhere in between – read on to discover more about yourself.

The Low-Sensitivity person: straight-talking, frank and outspoken

You're the kind of person who likes to speak your mind and get to the point. If people ask you for your opinion, you tell them what you think. If they ask you questions, you give your answer. Life's too short to waste time going round in circles. You prefer to say what you think. If you know that something is right or true, you'd much rather get it out into the open.

You are probably frustrated by people who won't tell you what they think, who shy away from sharing their opinions. When you ask a direct question, you'd appreciate an honest answer. But instead they skirt around the issue, bewildering the situation. Why won't they say what they want?

You're not frightened of making tough decisions, of taking a stance and standing up for it. You know that not everyone can be kept happy all of the time – that's just unrealistic. Sometimes you need to confront people. If they're doing something wrong, perhaps letting you or other people down, maybe making unreasonable demands, then why shouldn't you speak up? Someone needs to. If friends are making foolish decisions about their love lives, colleagues aren't pulling their weight or your children aren't eating their greens, they should be told. You feel compelled to speak the truth, to present the facts and set the situation right – even if that means a bit of disappointment, a few ruffled feathers or unpleasantness in the short term.

You hate to let others walk all over you, which can occasionally lead to a disagreement, a few heated words or an outright argument. But you sometimes relish the challenge of a good debate. And you'd rather be respected for having a view than be popular for saying nothing.

The High-Sensitivity person: diplomatic and tactful to the end

You're the sort of person who always knows how other people feel. But it goes deeper than that. When other people are feeling excited or depressed, angry or bored, you not only understand how they feel, but you *feel* that way too. Whether they're happy about getting a job offer or furious over an argument, you feel a little up or down with them as well.

You empathise with people so readily that putting yourself in others' shoes isn't just something you *can* do, it happens automatically. You can't help but know and appreciate how they feel.

Having such an exquisite attunement to other people's feelings means you're quick to spot what you have in common with people, rather than what separates you. You find it easier to agree than disagree. And when you have an opinion, you try to be diplomatic and tactful. You choose your words, your tone of voice, manner and timing with care. You don't want to offend anyone or put anyone out if you can help it. In fact, your whole nature is to be cooperative rather than combative.

When you come across people with difficult points of view, you instinctively tiptoe through the minefield of their emotions. And you're happy to be flexible. Because of the relationships you have with them, you're willing to give way, make concessions or even back down entirely. You do whatever it takes in the interests of preserving harmony.

You realise that putting everyone else first means that you sometimes come last. That you sometimes agree to more than you would have liked. That you may get saddled with the unsexy work assignment or a decision that wouldn't have been your first choice. But for the most part, you don't mind these things.

Make the most of yourself – for Low-Sensitivity people

What kind of a person do you think makes a good bailiff? Remember that bailiffs repossess furniture and goods from people who have maxed out their credit cards and can't pay their debts. So who would you hire for the job?

I watched a firm of bailiffs interview one particular candidate. Andrew stood at 6 foot 4 inches, he was built like a rugby player, spoke in a monosyllabic growl and was currently working as a nightclub bouncer. Oh, and he practised kickboxing in his spare time. The perfect candidate, right?

Wrong.

The firm of bailiffs turned him down. The boss explained to me that its best collection officer was in fact Brenda, a softly spoken 5 foot 2 inches woman in her late forties. That's because bailiffs aren't allowed to get physical. Contrary to the popular misconception that bailiffs are bruisers, they can't break down doors or push people around. Instead, Brenda charmed homeowners into opening the door so she could take away their 42-inch flatscreen TV, Xbox and sofa. She told people that she understood their situations and felt their pain. She persuaded potentially volatile people to let down their guard and let her in.

Taking the direct route doesn't always get results. Stating your requests and speaking your mind means that people always know where you stand. Trouble is, most people can simply say no.

Ask a debtor to hand over her DVD player and she can tell you to go to hell. Point out to a smoker that his cigarettes will kill him. Tell a colleague that the way he's doing something at work isn't the most efficient way. Or try explaining to your customers that they're making a mistake by not choosing your product. What do you think they will say? Will any of them thank you for your advice? Will any of them actually change their behaviour?

Probably not.

As a Low-Sensitivity person, you're the voice of reason, logic and rationality. The hitch is that most people are deeply illogical, emotional, unfathomable. You may be 'right' much of the time, but that doesn't mean people will listen. If you want to be more successful, to achieve more in your relationships with other people, you may need to take the indirect route at times. The suggestions given in this section show you how.

Understand the psychology of influence and persuasion

Telling the facts and explaining what you want doesn't always work. So what does?

Working with business leaders to help them become more successful, I get to observe a lot of managers in action. In one organisation – an investment business catering to wealthy individuals – the chairman is a self-made man who has grown the firm over two decades of hard work. But I spotted that ideas from his team often failed to impress him – even when they clearly had merit for the business.

The employees who succeeded in winning his support for projects and reaping the career rewards realised that business benefit was of only secondary importance. In order to succeed, they had to fan the flames of the chairman's ego. When I confronted him with my observation, he denied it at first. But as an outsider, I could see that an idea's benefit to the business without enough fan-waving was always doomed.

Like the chairman, most people have a hot button – a source of inner motivation that drives them and to which they respond. For some people it's money, pure and simple. For others it's popularity or status and the need to impress colleagues, friends or family. Others may seek security, to feel good in the eyes of God or to feel included as part of a team or family. It could be the need for recognition – to be appreciated as a great leader, a loving parent, an expert on a topic. Or maybe to have an easy, low-stress life.

Not everyone has the same motivation. And, to complicate matters, people sometimes have different motivations in different situations. You can bet, however, that few people are motivated purely by doing what is 'right' or 'best' in a situation.

High-Sensitivity individuals naturally get into the heads of other people to understand their motivations – what they yearn for, their hot buttons. But you can learn to do this too. Do it and you unlock the secrets to influencing and persuading the people around you.

Become your best: Uncovering people's hot buttons

People rarely talk about what motivates them unless they know you well enough to open up. Even then, many people aren't aware of their own true motivations – they may say one thing but mean another.

Your assignment is to figure out what motivates different people, what makes them tick. Imagine that you're a private detective who has been paid to work out the motivations of the key people in your life. Your ultimate goal is to put your findings into words and write a report. I suggest that you write at least a handful of bullet points for each person. Believing that you understand someone's motivations is very different from being confident enough to commit them to paper – even if it's for your eyes only.

Begin by making a list of half a dozen people who are important in your life and career – perhaps colleagues, your boss, family members. Then observe them and try to work out their hopes, fears, likes and dislikes. In particular, see if you can answer the following questions:

- When these people are presented with new ideas or proposals, what makes them agree to something? And what makes them say 'No'?
- What is each person passionate about?
- How would you describe each person's personality? Think of them on each of the seven personality dimensions within this book. Would you say that they were high, average or low scorers for each dimension? Write a short profile on your people and how they come across.
- What should you say or do to get them to say 'Yes'? How can you prepare and pave the way to increase your chances? What buttons do you need to push?

Over the days and weeks, collect evidence to back up your answers. What is it that each person does or says? How do their tones of voice alter when they're happy or displeased? How do their facial expressions betray their feelings?

Remember that the brain contains a series of pathways. This kind of mind-reading may not come so naturally to you, but the more you do it, the better you can get. So start now.

Learn to pull as well as push

A friend of mine, Craig, won't go to the dentist. He hasn't been to one for at least ten years. All of his friends – including myself – have argued that he should. We've warned him about the perils of tooth decay and gum disease. But will he listen to reason? Hell, no. The more we've tried to tell him, the more he's dug his heels in.

Telling people what to do rarely works. But you can still influence them and get them to change their minds. Generally speaking, you can either *push* people towards a goal or *pull* them towards it. You can push by telling people what to do, using authority or force of will or a rational argument to show them that they *should* or *must* behave a certain way. Or you can pull people towards your goal by inspiring and exciting them, and making them feel that they *want* to do what you suggest.

Take a look at the Talentspace ladder of influence below – a tool that I use at conferences and workshops to help audiences think about their impact and persuasiveness. The ladder begins at the bottom with 'push' influencing styles that are grounded in might and right, facts and figures and the right thing to do. Ascending to the top of the ladder you will find the 'pull' styles, which rely on lofty goals and ideas to inspire people into action. Of course we are capable of using all the different styles, but which do you think is your trademark style, the one that you currently use the most?

Most of us have a couple of dominant influencing styles. Many Low-Sensitivity people rely heavily on 'Convincing' and the

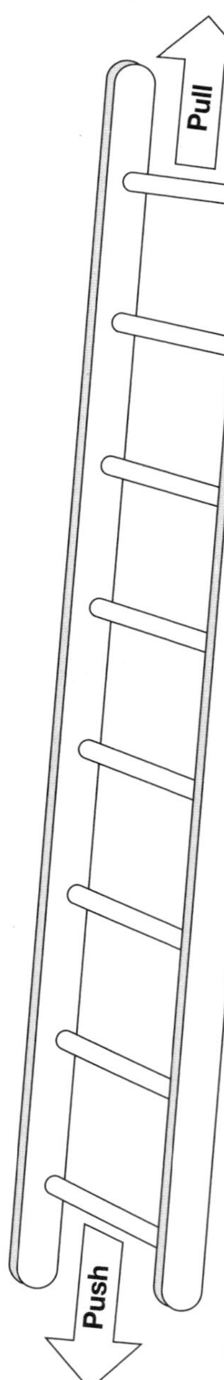

The Talentspace Ladder of Influence

Calling to action: Inspire people to act – speak passionately about a goal, paint a vivid picture of what can be done, engage people's emotions and appeal to their nobler instincts. Orators such as John F. Kennedy and Nelson Mandela epitomise this style.

Championing: Set a personal example for others by modelling a behaviour or activity. Walk the talk by being a role model and doing what you want others to do. Encourage people to change by demonstrating the benefits.

Coalition-building: Use third parties and a hint of peer pressure to influence others. Suppose Jane doesn't listen to you, but listens to Paul. So win Paul over and see if he can bring her round to your way of thinking. Even better, see if you can get three others onside to speak to Jane too.

Cajoling: Use warmth, charm, flattery and the friendship or rapport you have with people to beg a favour, twist their arm or otherwise persuade someone to do as you would like.

Collaborating: Work in total partnership with people to come up with a solution. True collaboration means going into discussions without an agenda. Be willing to consider all options rather than secretly having a solution that you hope to carry out.

Compromising: Look for a solution or outcome that at least partly meets everyone's needs. Make concessions and trade-offs to reach an agreement that all parties can live with.

Convincing: Use logical arguments, facts and figures, pros and cons to argue the merits of a case. Research your argument and explain the options you considered and discarded. Provide reasons people should do as you wish.

Commanding: Use authority or power to tell people what to do, even though they may have objections. Be strong during crises when quick, decisive action without lengthy discussion is needed.

Source: © Talentspace 2009, reprinted with permission.

other push styles towards the bottom of the ladder. High-Sensitivity people tend to rely too much on the pull styles.

No one style is inherently better than any other. If the fire alarm is going off and the building is filling with smoke, you don't have time to sit around, discuss how everyone feels and gain a consensus on how to evacuate the building – you need to take command. *Get everyone out*.

But when your organisation is introducing a new computer system and a different way of dealing with customers, you can't simply bark orders at people and expect them to do as they're told. You need to talk through the benefits, answer questions, make changes or even concessions if employees can come up with better suggestions. Work together to devise the best way forward. Yes, you could force them to do it your way, but that would create resentment and bad feelings, possibly derailing future attempts to get them on side.

Over to you

Think back to a recent time when you had a disagreement with someone. Reflect on the following questions:

- What happened?
- Which style(s) of influence did you deploy at the time?
- What other style(s) could you potentially have used?
- How would you handle the same situation if it happened again?

Influential people are chameleons – adaptable, flexible. They switch tactics constantly, reading different people and nuances in situations and changing styles as necessary.

What works to win over a customer during a negotiation may not be appropriate to persuade your mother-in-law not to buy you some hideous ornament for your birthday. What works to rally support for a charity may not have the desired effect when what you want is a favour from your boss.

The next time you need to influence an individual or change the minds of a group, which style are you going to use?

Become your best: Adding influencing styles to your repertoire

Expand your range of influencing styles by looking around you for individuals who exemplify each of the different methods. Who is the epitome of 'Call to action' or 'Collaborating' or whatever else you want to get better at? Once you've spotted such role models, work out what they say and do that makes them so effective.

You may know some of these people in person or perhaps have seen them on television or read about them in biographies or the press. Politicians, public figures, even Hollywood actors are often great examples of how (and sometimes how *not*) to influence and persuade others. Study them, observe them, read about them and the results they achieve. Scrutinise their every word and deed to see what you can incorporate into your own repertoire.

Uncover your own assumptions

"Assumptions are the termites of relationships."

Henry Winkler, actor

Say a friend or colleague lets you down. You emailed Paula last week asking her to book train tickets for Friday. She replied saying that she'd do it. But it's Friday now and guess what? She hasn't got the tickets. The facts are irrefutable – you even dug out the email exchange to check that she'd understood and agreed to your request. You'd be justified to point it out, even to tell her off for having messed up, right?

Well, *maybe*.

Become your best: Understanding how you attribute behaviour

If *other* people forget to do something, it's because they're lazy or careless. If *we* forget, it's because we're overworked or have other things on our minds. If *someone else* criticises us during a meeting, it's because she's trying to score points with the boss. If *we* point out a similar mistake, it's because we think that there are genuine lessons to be learned.

Psychologists have known for a long time that we typically attribute other people's mistakes to their personal failings, but attribute our own blunders to external circumstances. We give ourselves the benefit of the doubt, whereas we tend to find other people guilty straight away. But even when we think we know all of the facts, we usually don't. We simply can't know what other people were thinking, what they intended, what else was happening in their lives at the time.

Here's the lesson: *other people's thoughts and intentions are invisible.* You can *never* know what they're thinking. You are, all of the time, making assumptions based only on what you *think* you're seeing.

Without talking it over with Paula, you don't yet have the full picture. Perhaps she did book the tickets but the travel company lost her booking. Or the computer system may have gone down so she couldn't book the tickets. Maybe she did forget, but her daughter was taken into hospital at the beginning of the week. Or she was so inundated with work that she had been doing four or five hours of unpaid overtime every night for the past month. Perhaps she emailed you to say that she wouldn't be able to book the tickets, but the message got lost in the system. Maybe she couldn't book the tickets and she tried to tell you, but you were so busy that you didn't have time to listen.

For any situation, there are many possible explanations. *You can't know all of the facts.* So starting any difficult conversation with the 'facts' is likely to involve making assumptions about what actually happened. And that's a sure-fire way to make other people feel defensive. Before you know it, you're in a fully fledged argument, exchanging rash words, dredging up past misdemeanours and even engaging in personal attacks that may have little to do with what you actually wanted to discuss.

I'm not suggesting that you ignore the issue. Rather, think about your opening salvo, *how* you will approach the issue. Be clear that you are speaking only from your perspective and you don't yet have all the facts. Position the discussion very clearly as a conversation – a mutual exploration and fact-finding mission – rather than a telling-off.

The best way to broach any potentially difficult conversation is to talk about your feelings, to say that you feel let down, angry, shocked or whatever else you might be feeling. People may dispute the 'facts', but no one can argue about how you feel.

Become your best: Bringing your feelings to the fore

You need to point out a mistake, offer someone criticism or confront someone's behaviour. You get that you need to talk about your feelings, but here's another tip: be sure to start your statements in the first person singular ('I . . .') rather than the second person ('You . . .').

Avoid saying, '*You* excluded me from that discussion last week so I felt disappointed' because the other person could retort, 'I did not exclude you from that discussion!' Making 'you' statements assumes that you can read other people's minds about their intentions. It's safer to say, '*I* felt excluded from that discussion last week', with the implication, 'Regardless of whether you intended it or not, I felt that you excluded me from that discussion last week.'

Even when you feel that you have all the facts, choose to focus on your feelings. 'You didn't get the report out' is very direct, abrupt, almost accusatory. Instead, begin with, 'Can I share something with you? I feel rather disappointed and frustrated with a situation at the moment. Can I tell you my side of the story and see what you think?'

Talking about your feelings and inviting the other person to contribute gives you a much softer way into discussing the situation. Talking about your feelings allows you a much more conciliatory approach into difficult conversations.

Perhaps you're not convinced. Most people hate getting 'touchy feely'. I know a lot of people who would rather shovel cow manure than start a sentence with the words 'I feel ...' Especially at work, you may think that it's not appropriate to get into how you and everyone else feel.

But suppressing emotions just doesn't work. If you try to put on a front, they'll creep out anyway. We get cracks in the dam of our demeanour. Our emotions may leak into the tone of our voice, the set of our jaw, how we stand and hold ourselves. When we feel really strongly about something, angry words may fly or tears well up. Better to vent them in a controlled fashion by talking about them than pretend they don't exist and risk them bursting out when you least expect it.

You still get to broach the conversation. But rather than assuming you're right and the other person is wrong, you present the situation as an open-ended discussion in which you are simply trying to figure out what happened. Do that and you will get the best possible outcome.

Over to you

Have a go for yourself. Take a look at the following statements. At the moment they are potentially inflammatory comments that could ignite a confrontation, cause an argument. How could you turn them into invitations to jointly discuss the situation and find a solution?

- 'Why did you point out my mistake in front of the rest of the team?'
- 'You aren't doing enough of the housework. On top of my job, am I supposed to be our housekeeper too?'
- 'By continuing to argue against what the rest of us agreed, I think you're being rude and disruptive.'
- 'Your son has already put on so much weight because you're letting him eat too much junk food.'
- 'You promised that you were going to sort out the finances by the end of last week and you still haven't done it.'

I'll help you a bit. Here's how I might rephrase the first one. Rather than make such an accusation, a better opener might be, 'Do you have five minutes? Yes? I wanted to talk to you about the meeting this morning and get something off my chest. I felt really annoyed by something you said. I'd like to explain why I still feel annoyed and get your side of the story.'

How does that sound?

Now, I know you're probably thinking, 'That isn't how *real* people talk!'

You're right: most people don't talk like that. But just because you don't hear such language regularly doesn't make it any less powerful. Mediators use this language. Psychotherapists and marriage counsellors use this language. Diplomats and negotiators use this language. A small proportion of savvy leaders do too. Why not take a leaf out of their books? What's the worst that could happen if you try it? It doesn't work – yes, but you're no worse off and you can always go back to bludgeoning people with facts. But what's the *best* that could happen if you try?

No matter what your level of empathy, you can hone it further. Expand your emotional lexicon. In the same way that you get better at putting on the green with practice, you can get better at judging the right phrases and approach to use with another person.

Make the most of yourself – for High-Sensitivity people

You have an uncanny sense of how other people feel. Your empathy and willingness to put others first means that you're a great team player. That is a huge asset – at least *some* of the time.

I came across Polly and Shaun, 50:50 business partners in a start-up magazine publishing company. Polly is naturally high on Sensitivity. So when Shaun went through a tricky divorce, Polly was willing to take on some of his workload. When Shaun met a new partner and had a child, Polly again ended up taking on more of his workload. When the business struggled and cash was tight, she agreed to forgo her salary for a few months so Shaun could take a salary to support his young family.

Is Polly a team player? No doubt about it. But is she a doormat? Most of her friends have said on more than one occasion that she needs to stand up more for her rights.

People like Polly risk being less successful in their careers than other people. Research tells us that agreeable, High-Sensitivity people tend to earn less and progress more slowly up the ranks than their more straight-talking, Low-Sensitivity counterparts. I know, I know – there's more to life and happiness than money. But if you want to clamber up the ladder of career success and earn the big bucks, be aware that the best-paid jobs sometimes require toughness and the ability to make the hard decisions. To tell it how it is, say 'no' and disappoint others, even kick ass on occasion. So this section gives some advice on how you can do at least a little of that.

Facing up to the downside of empathy

You avoid conflict and disagreement because you want to make people happy. You probably don't mind putting their needs ahead of your own, even if it means more work and hassle for you. But what if putting their wants and needs first could be doing harm?

I see a pattern of behaviour developing when parents don't take a stand and set rules for their children. Spending a week on holiday with friends Charlotte and Daniel, I was amazed at the behaviour of their children. The children frequently talked – or even shouted – over the adults. And Charlotte and Daniel let them get away with it. Their ten-year-old daughter was sullen when their mother asked her to take some of the dinner plates into the kitchen. She took a few through to the kitchen then sat down in a huff, declaring, '*He* only had to carry three plates into the kitchen, why should I have to do any more?'

In their desire to be loved by their children, Charlotte and Daniel (and many other parents) are indulging their children. They're inadvertently creating me-me-me children who will turn into spoilt, selfish adults. As grown-ups, they will lack the give-and-take strategies to prosper in life.

The same goes at work too. Say a colleague is repeatedly turning up late for work and not doing his job properly. You know that he's suffering in the wake of difficulties at home and feel for him. You'd be inhuman not to sympathise. But what if his poor performance is putting customer relationships at risk? What if the other members of the team get so sick of picking up the slack that they decide to look for new jobs?

Willie Walsh, currently CEO of British Airways, was a mere week away from his fortieth birthday when he became CEO of Irish airline Aer Lingus. The airline was losing £2 million a day. His first task was to announce 2000 redundancies – a third of the workforce. How did he feel about that?

People say to me that it must have been hard to do that, because a lot of those people were my friends. But it wasn't, because I had no choice. Either a third of them went or all of them would have gone. It was that bad.

Sometimes you need to take a stand. To speak up when someone's idea is misguided, unrealistic, even dangerous. To take someone aside when she makes the same mistake over and over again, never learning from it. What if someone repeatedly fails to deliver on his commitments, makes a racist or sexist comment, or takes advantage of a colleague? What if someone flouts an important rule, disregards health and safety concerns, even breaks the law?

Stuart Goddard, divisional managing director at an investment boutique, put it to me this way:

Good people management is like good parenting. You need to balance kindness with toughness. Sometimes you should let things slide, but other times you need to be a firm disciplinarian so the problem doesn't get out of hand.

Polly Ford, owner of her own public relations firm, tells me:

You need to marry your heart with your head. Your heart may want to please people, but sometimes your head has to take action that's in the best interests of the team.

Over to you

By not speaking up, you risk doing others a disservice. You're assuming they're too fragile to be told the truth.

Think about your own situation for a moment. If you were doing something that was ineffective, a bit silly or plain wrong, wouldn't you want to be told? Say you cooked a dinner for friends and added far too much salt. Wouldn't you rather know to avoid doing it in future? If you were sending paperwork to the wrong department at work and creating more work for people, wouldn't you want them to say something? Or would you rather your friends and colleagues let you make the same old mistakes, time and time again, feeling more and more fed up every time you did it?

Putting other people's needs first isn't always a good thing. Identifying too strongly with their needs can harm the collective good or even them in the long term. So be careful if you have unruly children, friends or people in your team. How long are you willing to let them run riot?

"The art of leadership is saying no, not yes. It is very easy to say yes."

Tony Blair, former prime minister

Consider the best for everyone

No one is saying that your level of empathy is a bad thing. It's great that you can get into the heads of other people, experience the world from their perspective and feel how they feel. However, you mustn't let your empathy stop you from making the tough decisions. Decisions that may leave colleagues without a promotion, without the fun projects or the bonuses they covet. Decisions that may leave your children without the bag of sugary sweets they want to take to bed. Or your friend without the £10,000 investment he wants for his dubious new business venture.

You probably struggle to see when such decisions are necessary. Your gut reaction is to say 'yes' to people, to give in to their requests, to put them first. But sometimes you need to step back, appraise the situation and *not* automatically put others first. Here's a tried-and-tested technique to help you make the best decisions for everyone.

Become your best: Practising objective detachment

Objective detachment helps you to think about difficult circumstances from the perspective of a third party. What would an intelligent person who is not involved in the situation advise you to do? Imagine a judge in court listening to arguments and counter-arguments on behalf of a plaintiff and defendant(s).

Work through the following steps:

1 **Write down the other person's situation.** Think of this person as a plaintiff in court, making some kind of request. Jot down a handful of bullets to capture the other person's behaviour and situation – what he or she has said or done to date.

2 **Write down your and others' needs.** These others are the defendants in this situation. But the first person you need to think about is *you*. What would *you* ideally like to get out of the situation? Then consider your colleagues, customers, family, friends, whoever. Your aim here is to take into account the collective good. Write a couple of sentences for each person or group.

3 **Consider the plaintiff's role.** In other words, what is generally expected of a person who is an employee, a supplier, daughter, husband, *boss*? Would you expect most employees to turn up to work drunk? Suppliers to deliver their shipments late? Daughters to be rude to their grandparents? Your aim here is to maintain a distance between yourself and your current situation. Think about what the average person would expect of a person in that role.

4 **Imagine a judge in court listening to the arguments and counter-arguments.** What would a judge declare needs to happen in your situation? What's the best solution for everyone?

By spending a few minutes setting your thoughts out on paper, you can weigh your options up properly and make decisions that *don't* automatically put the other person first. But it only works if you use it! Having it at the back of your mind isn't good enough.

If a friend or colleague catches you with a request, ask for time to think about it. By all means listen to the request, but avoid making a decision there and then. Say, 'I need a little time to think about it. Give me X minutes/hours/days.' Then take those minutes or hours or days to write down your thoughts, divorcing your immediate feelings from the right thing to do. If you allow yourself to be bullied into making decisions on the spot, you are much more likely to capitulate, to give in to other people's demands and regret it later.

Over to you

Think about a person that you would like to be more assertive with. Perhaps something has happened in the past that you want to bring up. Maybe something is going on right now. Write down the answers to the following questions:

- What are the *advantages* of speaking up?
- What are the *disadvantages* of not saying anything?
- What's the *best* that could happen if you speak up?
- When and where would be a good time and place to raise the issue with this person?
- What will you actually say? Write down the first few sentences you will actually use to broach the topic. Then recite them out loud a couple of times to get more comfortable saying them.

Tell it straight

The advantage of being a High-Sensitivity individual is that you're good at talking about your feelings. As I advised Low-Sensitivity people earlier in this chapter, that's the single best way to kick off a discussion when you want to give someone feedback.

That said, Low-Sensitivity people tend to be better at stating their case, at talking about their perspective. The challenge for many High-Sensitivity people is that they don't like to assert themselves, to put forward their point of view. But it is easy to learn how.

Become your best: Giving effective feedback

When people are evidently going wrong, you need to speak up. Remember that you're doing them a disservice by not giving them proper guidance. Criticism need not be confrontational or cataclysmic if you follow the '7 Cs' of effective feedback:

- **Clear.** Prepare what you want to say ahead of time. Most people find it easier to deliver a message that they've thought about than have to think on their feet. Five minutes of planning is all it takes.
- **Current.** Give feedback as soon as possible after a situation has arisen. The longer you let it linger, the more ingrained the problem becomes. Effective feedback is timely, not left for months until the annual appraisal.
- **Candid.** You owe it to both yourself and the other person to be honest. If you feel a certain way about something, you should say so. Hiding how you feel means that you end up skirting around the issue and never resolving it properly.
- **Consequential.** Explain the consequences or impact of the situation or the other person's behaviour. It's not enough to say, 'You are entering data into the spreadsheet incorrectly'. You need to point out how it affects you or other people: '. . . which means that I have to spend an extra hour rechecking all of the numbers before I can do my job.'
- **Constructive.** Pointing out what someone has done wrong is a start. But together you should aim to find a solution rather than simply use

the mistake to beat someone up repeatedly. What suggestions do you have as to how the other person could behave differently in the future?

- **Confidence-building.** Effective feedback should aim to correct someone's behaviour and resolve the situation, but a lot of it ends up making people feel bad about themselves. Instead, bolster the person's mood and confidence by helping the individual to consider the feedback in the broader context of what he or she does well.
- **Consistent.** Be sure to treat all of the people around you equally. If you point out one person's mistakes but not another's, you will be accused of having favourites. So be consistent in applying the same rules to everyone in the team or family.

ONWARDS AND UPWARDS

Sometimes we need greater empathy; sometimes we need detachment. Remember that it's neither better nor worse to be low or high on Sensitivity. Low-Sensitivity people could at times do with being more tactful; High-Sensitivity people need to be more direct on occasion.

Here's a quick reminder of words and phrases that broadly distinguish people who are at either end of the spectrum.

Low-Sensitivity	High-Sensitivity
Usually direct and to the point.	Usually diplomatic and considerate.
Good at confronting poor performance.	Good at making people feel understood.
Focus too much on the facts of a situation.	Focus too much on other people's feelings.

Low-Sensitivity cont.	High-Sensitivity cont.
May be criticised for being too blunt, abrasive.	May be criticised for dodging issues.
Too assertive – may be seen as aggressive.	Not assertive enough – may be seen as weak.
Need to talk about their feelings ('I feel . . .') more.	Need to consider the facts ('I think . . .') more.

If you scored lower on Sensitivity:

- Recognise that few people are swayed by facts alone. Telling people the 'right' course of action is rarely enough to change their behaviour. Keep in mind the different – particularly 'pull' – influencing styles that you can deploy in persuading people to your way of thinking.
- Appreciate that most people – including you – make certain assumptions when they engage in potentially difficult discussions. Be sure to explain that you want to share your side of the story but you don't have the whole picture yet.
- Get used to talking about your feelings. Pretending that feelings don't exist means that they may burst forth anyway. The simple words 'I feel . . .' can defuse conflict and put you and others on a collaborative rather than confrontational footing.
- Play to your strengths for long-term success. Seek out environments in which your honesty and directness are appreciated. Find bosses and colleagues and friends who genuinely want you to tell it as it is and not as they want it.

If you scored higher on Sensitivity:

- Recognise that *not* speaking up can be more harmful in the long term than giving someone your honest opinion. Remember how you'd feel if you were doing something badly or making a mistake – wouldn't *you* want to know?

- Consider how an objective third party would regard your situation. If you were advising a friend or a judge were appraising the state of affairs, what would they say needs to happen?
- Spend a few minutes working through the '7 Cs' of effective feedback. Planning what you want to say helps you to get your message across assertively yet tactfully.
- Succeed in the long term by seeking out situations and organisations that allow you to work collectively and collaboratively. Avoid ones in which you will be constantly required to challenge people and fight your corner.

07

Knowledge Questing

"Learning is not compulsory . . . neither is survival."

W. Edwards Demming, author

How did you like school – or, more precisely, the studying, homework, exams?

One friend from my school days struggled to learn foreign languages. School policy was that everyone was to take exams in at least two languages, but Martin dropped them as quickly as he could. The moment he finished the exams, he invited his friends out to celebrate that he would never have to pick up a French dictionary or Latin textbook again. Hurrah!

But another of my mates, Ian, couldn't get enough of languages. He took French, Spanish, German and Latin. The school only allowed us to take a maximum of four languages, but he studied ancient Greek and Russian in his own time – *and* decided to take exams in them too! Unsurprisingly, he went on to study languages at university and completed a doctorate in linguistics.

For Martin, studying languages was something he *had* to do to get through school. Like having wisdom teeth extracted, it was painful but necessary. For Ian, languages weren't a chore. They weren't something he studied simply to pass exams; they represented his passion. He loved to learn.

Martin and Ian represent the two ends of the Knowledge Questing spectrum. Knowledge Questing is a measure of people's love of learning for its own sake. Some people (like Martin) shy away from courses and formal education. They'd much rather focus on the work they have to do than waste time studying. Others (like Ian) get fired up and excited by reading, going on courses and accumulating qualifications – they can't get enough of learning. Where do you sit on the Knowledge Questing spectrum?

Your Knowledge Questing

Review Questionnaire 6, back on page 14. Award yourself two points each time you agreed with one of the statements numbered 1, 2, 4, 5, 7 and 9. Add to your tally two points each time you disagreed with any of the statements numbered 3, 6, 8 and 10. You should have a score between 0 and 20.

A score of 8 or less suggests that you're low for Knowledge Questing. A score of 16 or more suggests that you are high for Knowledge Questing. A score of between 10 and 14 means that you have average levels of Knowledge Questing.

Remember that in working through the rest of this chapter, you only need to read the sections that are aimed at your personality profile. Generally speaking, the advice within the Low-Knowledge Questing section may be helpful for average scorers too.

What kind of person are you?

Knowledge Questing is fundamentally about people's love of (or aversion to) formal learning and education. Some people are drawn to books, courses, even exams, while others shy away from them.

High-Knowledge Questing people are book-smart and succeed by pursuing traditional forms of education. Low-Knowledge Questing people prefer to learn by doing. Neither is inherently better. Bear in mind that some incredibly successful people dropped out of school or university (including Academy award-winning director Stephen Spielberg, editor-in-chief of *Vogue* magazine, Anna Wintour, and founder of Virgin, Richard Branson).

Whether you scored low or high on Knowledge Questing, remember that people succeed in work and life from both ends of the spectrum. Success and fulfilment come from recognising your unique strengths and finding situations that fit you well.

The Low-Knowledge Questing person: you'd rather do it than read about it

You're a busy person with lots to do. You can be forgiven for preferring to get on with the stuff you need to do – the work at hand – than go on a course or pick up a book to read about some theory. Sure, in an ideal world you'd have enough free time to study and go on courses. But you feel that you simply have too much to do in your day-to-day job and life.

If you're faced with a problem, you ask someone for help, you don't pick up a book about it. You learn by talking it over with someone you know or observing someone in the real world, not by attending a seminar or training programme. Acquire a new computer, mobile, washing machine or any piece of technology and you want to give it a go, not wade through the manual or handbook.

On those rare occasions you do get sent on a course, you want the trainer to get to the point! You probably hate the theory and want to know how you can use it in your day-to-day work. And while you're there, do you spend a fair chunk of the time thinking about how you'd much rather be at your desk, doing your job?

You probably realise that you're not a fan of training and formal education. Perhaps the pattern was set in your school days. You hated the rote learning, the coursework and exams of your formative years. It's hardly surprising, then, that you see formal education as something to be endured rather than enjoyed.

The High-Knowledge Questing person: learn, learn, learn!

You love to learn. You look at the world around you and want to know more about everything. You probably have a dozen books and articles on the go at the same time. Perhaps you have a list of courses or qualifications you'd like to pursue too.

People like you enjoy studying and do well at exams. So perhaps you're in a profession such as law, medicine or accountancy. If not, you probably find ways to read up outside of your work.

Whatever your walk of life, you read voraciously about new developments and get filled with excitement about them – you want to try them out. You're often one of the first to become a fan and advocate of new books, ideas, techniques, films and maybe even gadgets. In tech terms, you're what's known as an early adopter, the kind of person who passionately embraces new tools and evangelises about them to others. Perhaps not in every field of life or every kind of technology, but you probably delight in being at the forefront in at least certain areas. As a result, you may have developed a bit of a reputation as the expert on those topics.

No one ever has to force you to attend a seminar or go on a training workshop. You value education and see it as a vital part of your development, of keeping up to date in your field or profession. Your only wish would be that you had more time and money to go on even more courses!

Make the most of yourself – for Low-Knowledge Questing people

I can fully understand if you don't enjoy classrooms and going on courses. If you feel that picking up a book or business magazine is the last thing you want to do after a long day at work, that's perfectly natural.

But here's the bad news: it's a competitive, fast-moving world out there – and it's only getting faster.

Maybe 20 or even 10 years ago we could rely on taking a job with one employer and gradually climbing the career ladder. On having more or less the same skill set and waiting for our bosses to tell us what skills we needed to get to the next rung. But that's not the way of the world any more.

Keep an eye on the future

"It is not the strongest of the species that survives, nor the most intelligent that survives. It is the one that is most adaptable to change."

Charles Darwin, naturalist

The twin forces of technology and globalisation mean that jobs are changing. Some 20 years ago we didn't have iPods or DVDs, stem cells or keyhole surgery or even laptop computers and the Internet. There weren't jobs with titles such as 'web designer' or 'call centre manager', 'life coach' or even 'pole dancer'! The boardroom didn't have chief technology officers, heads of human capital management, chief information officers. Another ten years from now, we'll have another slew of completely new jobs.

Think about your job, your organisation. Research by the Chartered Institute of Personnel and Development found that most organisations undergo major change *at least* once every three years. Your organisation has probably restructured or downsized a handful of times in the last few years. Departments get closed and new ones started up. Everyone's duties and work are thrown up in the air. Perhaps new people are taken on, while people who don't cut it get fired.

Change is happening – and it's happening fast. Want to know more? Have a look at some of the following resources by top business strategists and future-focused writers:

- *The Future of Management* by Gary Hamel (Harvard Business School Press, 2007)
- *A Whole New Mind* by Daniel Pink (Marshall Cavendish, 2008)

- the annual 'Breakthrough Ideas' issue of *Harvard Business Review* (available online at: http://hbr.harvardbusiness.org)
- *Fast Company* magazine (available online at: www.fastcompany.com).

Over the years, I've worked with many successful executives and leaders in their fields. And I can tell you that savvy people keep an eye on the future, on shifts and approaching upheavals in the world. They spot a trend and decide to investigate further. They realise that everyone else is getting excited about the environment, the economy, advances in biotechnology, software, hardware or whatever. Then they take steps to learn more. Because *knowing* the future will be different isn't enough – you have to understand it and get yourself there too.

Don't just take my word for it. Jenny Ungless is an executive search consultant at Ellwood & Atfield. She's hired by major corporations and government organisations to scout out high achievers with outstanding track records. She said:

> *In my experience, people who are at the top of their game are better informed. They have interests in politics, technology, history, sport, the world at large and not only their own branch of industry. High performers don't just deal with the urgent day-to-day stuff that clamours for their attention, such as clearing their inboxes. They set time aside to invest in reading and speaking to a wide range of people, which ultimately pays off massively.*

I saw on the Discovery channel that sharks need to keep swimming 24 hours a day, moving forwards all of the time to keep fresh water passing over their gills. They never stop. Fish, on the other hand, are quite content to sit still, switch off for a while and doze off. In the struggle for survival, who would you bet on? The shark or the fish? If you don't keep moving, you'll be chewed up, spat out and left behind.

So don't be so guilty of working *in* your job – doing the day-to-day tasks that your job requires of you – that you neglect to work *on* your job. If you don't work on your long-term prospects, who else is going to?

Over to you

You probably already have a niggling idea of the kind of reading and learning that you need to do. Perhaps you've been putting it off for a while. Off the top of your head, what are the three topic areas that you know you really should be learning more about? Write them down here.

- ....
- ....
- ....

Look ahead

A friend of mine, Susannah, was recently made redundant. She was a hard worker and good at her job, but profitability had been sliding for a couple of years within the division where she worked. Even a series of new division heads had failed to turn its fortunes around. Ultimately, the organisation's overlords closed down the entire division, firing the 40 or so employees so they could focus on the rest of the business.

Could Susannah have prevented it? Probably not. But should she have seen it coming and prepared a way to jump before she was pushed? Absolutely.

The lesson? Avoid focusing so intently on the here and now, what's right under your nose, that you miss what's coming up. We all get so inundated by our work. We get our heads down to tackle the huge pile of work and can lose sight of the bigger picture. So unlike Susannah, make sure that you lift your head occasionally and look out for new trends tools, techniques, tactics, advances and ways of working to keep ahead of the pack.

Become your best: Completing a personal PESTLE

I appreciate that you're busy, but this exercise mainly involves talking to people. Before you do that, though, jot down the following headings on a blank sheet of paper:

- Political
- Economic
- Social
- Technological
- Legal
- Environmental

You will see that the first letters of these words spell 'PESTLE'. Now put the sheet of paper to one side, making a mental note to return to it later.

Over the next few weeks, make an effort to read and talk to people about what's going on in the world. Once you set your mind to paying attention to the political, economic, social, technological, legal and environmental changes that are going on in the world, you will find it very easy to accumulate information for each category.

After a couple of weeks, return to your sheet of paper and jot down your thoughts. What are the trends and changes that are happening in the world or your industry? Some of these could affect your organisation or department. But what you're ultimately looking to identify are the opportunities and threats that could affect *you* in the foreseeable future.

It doesn't matter if you can't decide whether a particular change or trend should go into one category or another. Should a growing proportion of pensioners be classified as a political challenge or a social one? Really doesn't matter. Just write it down.

Once you've collected your thoughts on the PESTLE changes that could affect you in the next few years, ask yourself: 'What do I need to *do* about all of this?'

Crafting your personal PESTLE isn't a precise science. At first, the results may seem obvious – you kind of knew what would come out of it all along. Problem is, that stuff is only ever 'obvious' after it's been pointed out. We miss so-called 'obvious' events all the time because we're too busy focusing on the tasks and hassles of our daily lives.

I'll give you an example. James Deakin runs a ten-strong plumbing business and does an annual PESTLE. Several years ago, when the European Union expanded to include Poland, he realised that Polish plumbers would soon arrive who would be willing to undercut him on price. So he had the foresight to visit Poland to recruit a handful of the most skilled plumbers.

In last year's PESTLE, he spotted that many Polish tradespeople have been going home. So he took on a couple of young local apprentices. Initially, the apprentices cost him more than they earned, plus they sucked up his time. But now he tells me that there's a dearth of good plumbers around and he's nicely positioned, with his nearly qualified team of young plumbers, to grow the business and make a tidy sum.

Doing a personal PESTLE involves thinking strategically *about your own life*. No one is saying that you have to dream up a grand strategy for your organisation or industry. Unless you're the boss of the organisation, leave that to someone else. This is just about investing a couple of hours of your time, once a year, to look ahead and make sure you don't get left behind. Can you do that?

Seek a mentor

I play tennis. I started playing regularly a couple of years ago, but I quickly noticed that I wasn't very good. I kept losing. A lot. I'd never had lessons when I was a kid. Other players rolled their eyes when it was their turn to take me on as their doubles partner. Never mind, eh?

Well, no, actually. I did mind. I wanted to improve. So I asked one of the better players there, Keith, to teach me a bit. Over several months we met up a handful of times. I booked a court and he graciously gave me his time and his wisdom. And it made all the difference. I learned exactly how high to toss the ball in the air and when to hit it as it came down. I learned to move my feet in one way for a forehand but another way for a backhand. A few hours of advice made more difference to my game than the many dozens of hours I'd been playing.

If you want to get better at anything, see if you can find someone to counsel you. Whether it's a sport, a technical discipline or a work-related skill, find someone who can point out where you're going wrong and how you could be better. While High-Knowledge Questing people are often happiest attending courses or picking up books, Low-Knowledge Questing individuals often learn best from other people.

A mentor may be older and more experienced than you. Sometimes not. Sure, I have a doctorate in psychology. But I've learned loads about one new field in psychology from a younger psychologist studying for a specialist diploma who has not only the knowledge but also the enthusiasm to bring me up to speed. I once had a mentor from within the same organisation who had only 18 months more time in the job than me. She had more experience, but could still remember what it felt like to be the newcomer.

A mentor can pass on job or life skills or help you to navigate the choppy waters and politics at work. They can tell you about gaffes others have made and what it takes to make things happen, who to ask for help and who to avoid. They can even tell you about gaps in your CV that could hinder your unbridled ascent.

Now, you might be wondering, 'Why on earth would a busy, successful person agree to help and advise you?' Well, let me flip the question around. Imagine someone at work says to you,

'I've been reading some of your reports and think they're sensational. Wonderfully well written and interesting. Could I please buy you lunch and ask you how you've become such a great writer?' Would you send that colleague away or be flattered and try to explain what you do?

You can learn from a mentor and it won't even feel like work. Trust me when I tell you that you need one. The only thing is, don't expect a mentor to come knocking on your door. *You* have to take responsibility for finding one. Are you ready to find a mentor?

Become your best: Finding a mentor (or two or three ...)

Here's a step-by-step guide to finding (and keeping) a mentor:

- **Evaluate the field.** A mentor should be someone who has knowledge and/or influence, certainly. But, more than that, he or she must be someone you respect. Of course you may dream of being mentored by Richard Branson or Bill Clinton. But you will have a better chance if you target people who inhabit the same kind of world as you. A good rule of thumb is to look for people who have the careers and lives that you realistically believe you could achieve in say five to ten years' time.
- **Plan your approach.** Before you meet with a prospective mentor, invest a little thought in what your career and life goals are. What do you hope to get out of the mentoring? How often would you like to meet? What might you be able to offer in return?
- **Just ask.** Sometimes the direct route is the best approach. Make an appointment and ask if he or she will mentor you. Explain that you admire their success and want to learn from them.
- **Treat your mentor as a prized resource.** Your mentor may have great wisdom and a wealth of contacts, but don't simply turn up for a

mentoring session and expect your mentor to tell you what you should be doing to succeed. You must take responsibility for setting the agenda. Be sure to prepare before each mentoring session to make the best of the limited time you have together. Choose carefully the decisions and strategic issues you want your mentor's opinion on.

Be flexible in how you learn from mentors. Some mentors may agree to meeting with you just once. Others may agree to meeting with you on a semi-regular basis – perhaps every few months or a couple of times a year. And why restrict yourself to only one mentor? No single person is likely to know everything that you need to know, so why not have a handful of mentors to cover all the different topics you want to learn more about?

A survey by management consultants McKinsey & Company in 2008 found that 34 per cent of executives reported having been influenced by a mentor in their careers. To me, that says that two-thirds of executives are making life really tough for themselves. So the choice is yours. Do you want to make it easy or really difficult for yourself? Stupid question, right? Go get yourself a mentor.

Over to you

Any idea who might be willing to mentor you? The only criteria are that: (a) you rate their knowledge and success and (b) you respect them enough to listen to them. If you've done your personal PESTLE analysis, you should have a good idea of the topics or skill areas that you need to work on. Who could help you with those? Write down the names of three potential mentors now.

- ....
- ....
- ....

Of course, you may have reservations about approaching these people. They're perhaps older, more experienced, wiser, more successful. The worst that could happen is that they say no. On the other hand, think about the *best* that could happen – you might just gain someone quite amazing to guide, teach and advise you.

Make the most of yourself – for High-Knowledge Questing people

I'm coaching Laurie, who scored very high on Knowledge Questing. She has qualifications in psychology, hypnotherapy, neuro-linguistic programming, counselling and thought field therapy. A prodigious reader, she consumes two or three books a week and is currently studying for a master's degree in yet another branch of psychology. When I introduced her to the discipline of psychometric testing, her immediate impulse was to become qualified in that too. Oh, and she does all this while running her own business to boot.

Her approach has its advantages – she definitely knows more about recent advances in psychology than I do. However, all of that learning and her unquenching thirst for knowledge means that she lacks focus. She skips from one topic to the next; she never quite beds one down before getting lured by the next. Her biggest challenge – and I keep reminding her of it – is to turn her academic knowledge and qualifications into useful products with which she can build her business. Knowledge without application is wasted.

You are someone who finds pleasure in learning, reading about new areas and perhaps even accumulating qualifications. You absorb knowledge quickly and, quite frankly, you almost certainly know more than the people around you. But what do you *do* with all that knowledge?

Beware the curse of knowledge

Our household gained a new, furry-faced family member over the summer – a gregarious schnauzer puppy. We decided to call him Byron. Before his arrival, I read up on the breed. I bought books and read them with a highlighter pen. I joined online forums to ask questions of other schnauzer owners. I made a schedule for his meals, when to take him out to do his business in the garden, when to get his vaccinations, when to begin his puppy classes. I read that puppies have to be exposed to other dogs and new situations before they're too old (16 weeks of age, to be precise) to ensure they grow up into well-adjusted dogs. I even took time off work to train him in those early vital weeks.

The good news is that he's become a remarkably gregarious, outgoing dog. Full of life, fun-loving, yet obedient. I take pride in the fact that we brought him up so well.

The downside is that, boy, am I now a know-it-all when it comes to dogs. Probably unbearably so. When friends mention in passing that they're thinking of getting a dog, I bombard them with information on house training, vaccinations, breed selection, the quality of different puppy foods, vet fees, training practices. The list goes on.

I can't help it – or at least I couldn't to start with. I wanted to help, to make sure they made the right decisions. But then I learned to bite my tongue, to shut up. I realised that I was coming across as bossy, big-headed and a know-it-all!

Being too well read or well informed is the curse of knowledge. Like most High-Knowledge Questing people, you frequently *do* know more. You yearn to steer others in their thinking, tell them where they're going wrong, help them to avoid pitfalls that you can see so clearly. A walking thesaurus-cum-encyclopaedia, you have an opinion and you're usually right. However, the truth of the matter, is that most people rarely appreciate advice. Most people would prefer to go on in blissful ignorance than have someone point out their mistakes.

I know that sounds strange to you, but then you're not like most people. You scored high for Knowledge Questing – you *want* to seek out more information and knowledge. Most of the people around you are either low or average on Knowledge Questing.

Ever heard of the saying, 'Don't shoot the messenger'? Well, the messenger frequently does get shot. If you're the one pointing out to people that they're making a bad decision, you'll get both barrels emptied into your chest. Maybe not directly. They may tell you that they are grateful you pointed out the issue so they can fix it. But secretly, they may resent you, believe you're interfering and think you should mind your own business.

I know that sounds harsh, but unsolicited advice is rarely welcome.

Become your best: Choosing your moments to get involved

You know more than most. You can see where they're going wrong and you want to help. But before you open your mouth, consider whether your opinions are really necessary. Here are a few questions to help you decide how best to phrase your thoughts – or even whether to speak up at all:

- **Does it *really* matter?** Is someone about to make a life-altering decision or a major mistake? If someone is doing something that's 'good enough', does it matter if the way they're doing it isn't as perfect as you know it could be?
- **Would staying silent enable others to learn and grow?** Sometimes the best lessons in life are learned when people find their own solutions rather than when they've simply been told what to do.
- **Could you ask a question rather than make a comment?** Rather than saying, 'There's a more up-to-date piece of that software

available at the moment', perhaps you could ask, 'If there's a more up-to-date piece of software available at the moment, would you be interested or wouldn't it matter?'

No one likes a smart ass. Sometimes the best way to prove you're smart is by *not* saying what you secretly know.

Leave the learning behind

Don't expend too much of your energy on staying up to date in your field and working to improve your technical brilliance. The higher up the career ladder you climb, the less your technical expertise matters. I work with a leading law firm and the partners willingly admit that they know less about the law than the younger lawyers who work for them. As they move from being junior associates to senior partners, they say that the work changes from being one of deciphering technical legalese to managing client relationships and leading the team.

Rodney Marsh, who heads an educational think-tank, puts it this way:

> *I know this makes me sound like a loser, but my ideal Monday morning would be reading White Papers and journal articles. But when I've got 40-plus people looking to me for guidance, I know that's not the smartest use of my time.*

That's probably true in most professions. Move into management – whether you're managing a team of engineers or nurses, salespeople or computer programmers – and your greatest challenges are increasingly to do with other people. Your job as a manager and leader is to supervise, delegate, coach and manage relationships, to develop your team and liaise with the outside world. Leave the technical stuff to the team.

While reading more and going on courses are worthy goals, consider how else you could more profitably invest your time. You only have 24 hours in the day. An hour poring over a technical manual is one less hour you have in the day. Think about putting your time to best use. Rather than wading through a technical or business journal for an hour, could you spend it strengthening relationships and finding out about customer needs? Or having coffee with a colleague and figuring out how to work together more effectively?

Become your best: Focusing and following through

Given the rate at which you absorb information and knowledge about the world, you probably have an answer to most questions or an opinion on most topics. But the question is do you *apply* it? Do you turn each article or book you read, every course or lecture you attend, into something that you can exploit in your work or your life?

Many High-Knowledge Questing people spread themselves too thinly. They get too excited by what's coming up on the horizon and don't give enough attention to following through on the knowledge they already have.

Before embarking an *another* course, qualification or even book or article, consider the following:

- **Have you applied the last thing you learned?** Have you turned the theory into practice – not just once or twice, but enough times for your investment to have paid off?
- **How will you use the next piece of knowledge in your work or life?** Are there direct benefits? If not, should you be investing your time in something that's more hands-on?
- **What are the costs?** What are the financial consequences of embarking on that course or buying another book? Apart from the money side, how much of your *time* would this take up?

- **Does your best friend think it's a good idea?** Given your tendency to chase novelty, ask people who know you well for an opinion. Then *listen* to that opinion, even if they give you the answer you'd rather *not* hear!

ONWARDS AND UPWARDS

Learning and bettering yourself is a good thing – in moderation. Low-Knowledge Questing individuals could do a little more, but High-Knowledge Questing people could do a little less.

Here's a reminder of how Low- and High-Knowledge Questing people broadly differ.

Low-Knowledge Questing	High-Knowledge Questing
Shy away from courses and classrooms.	Put themselves forward for courses.
Avoid exams and qualifications.	Enjoy exams and gaining qualifications.
See studying as a chore.	See studying as a pleasure.
Prefer to learn by doing and observing others.	Prefer to learn through traditional forms of education.
May focus too much on today's demands.	May focus too much on the far-flung future.
Need to read and learn more.	Need to do more hands-on activities.

If you scored lower on Knowledge Questing:

- Recognise that our rapidly changing world throws up both threats and opportunities. The skills and knowledge you need tomorrow may not be the same as the ones you have today.

- Look for ways to learn in short bursts rather than go on long courses. Definitely steer clear of professions that expect you to study for exams!
- Analyse the world around you by considering the PESTLE trends and changes that could affect your life and ability to earn a living. What are the gaps in your CV and how might you go about filling them?
- Find someone you respect to mentor you. Keep asking until you find someone (or more than one person) who can guide you, help you with some of the bigger decisions and point you in the right direction.

If you scored higher on Knowledge Questing:

- For long-term success and fulfilment, seek out situations that allow – or even insist on – continuous learning and development. Avoid jobs that expect you simply to repeat the same way of doing things day in, day out.
- Bear in mind that no one likes a know-it-all. Yes, you are probably right more often than not, but people resent being told that they're wrong or not as clued up as they thought they were.
- Be aware that telling people the answer means they lose the opportunity to develop their problem-solving skills and knowledge. Learn to hold back your advice so that others can learn and grow.
- Consider the opportunity cost of books and articles, courses and seminars. Classroom and book learning are essential in the early stages of a career, but should increasingly give way to hands-on involvement with customers and colleagues as you progress upwards.

Drive

"The only place where success comes before work is in a dictionary."

Vidal Sassoon, hairdressing magnate

You have goals in life. You want to make more of yourself, achieve more and get ahead. You wouldn't have picked up this book otherwise. But exactly how hungry are you to succeed? What are you willing to do to achieve your goals? How many personal sacrifices are you prepared to make?

I work with a law firm, helping the senior partners to coach and develop young lawyers with the potential to be the partners of the future. Several years ago, the law firm chose a group of around 20 high-flyers to receive special coaching from me. Among even this super-talented and ambitious group, one of them stood out. When the firm's official coaching programme ended, Adam decided to carry on. He wanted extra coaching, paying for it out of his own pocket.

Whenever he was up for promotion, he asked for help in preparing for the interview panel. We worked on his leadership skills, his presence, demeanour with clients, everything – because he yearned to be word perfect and a superb leader.

He worked hard. Oh, so hard. On top of whatever was required of him, he took on countless additional projects to get noticed by the senior partners. He ran graduate recruitment fairs, organised client parties, arranged management away-days, spoke at business forums, trained junior lawyers. That meant he usually worked 80 or 90 hours a week. Just so you know, a 90-hour week means working 8 a.m. till midnight, *six* days a week.

And he has made it. In his mid-thirties, he's not only one of the youngest partners but also the chief operating officer – second-in-command to the managing partner at one of the country's fastest-growing law firms. Earning somewhere in the mid-six figures a year, his experience and profile ensure that he can take his pick of law jobs probably anywhere in the world.

Contrast High-Drive Adam with William. A long-standing friend, William is a talented graphic designer. He has been told on more than one occasion that he should apply for an internal promotion, but he doesn't want to manage other people. He's been offered jobs elsewhere, but he hates interviews and doesn't like taking risks. That frustrates me and a lot of his friends. We believe in him and know he could achieve more, but he's not bothered. Yes, he'd like to earn more, but he's mostly content with his lot. Ultimately, he's happy to be a part of the team rather than the boss of one.

Drive is the personality dimension that taps into your desire to succeed. It's the extent to which you need to compete, win, achieve, take charge, claw your way up the career ladder and get ahead. So how about you? Whether you're a go-getting Adam or a happy-go-lucky William – or somewhere in between – let's explore how you can get more out of your life.

Your Drive

Take a look back at Questionnaire 7 on page 16. Give yourself two points for agreeing with any of these statements: 1, 3, 4, 6, 9 and 10. And give yourself two points for disagreeing with any of these statements: 2, 5, 7 and 8. You should have a score between 0 and 20.

A score of 8 or less suggests that you are a Low-Drive individual. A score of 14 or more means that you are a High-Drive person. A score of between 10 and 12 means that you have medium levels of Drive.

You know the drill by now. Pick out the sections within this chapter that are aimed at your personality profile. If you sit in the middle on Drive, read both sets of descriptions and cherry-pick the advice that seems most suited to your situation.

What kind of person are you?

All of us are driven to a certain extent. Some are highly driven and others a little less so. Whatever your level of Drive, you face both challenges and opportunities. Let's explore how you can get more out of life and find your own brand of fulfilment.

The Low-Drive person: at ease with your life and career

You're someone who understands the need for a balance between work and life. To you, having a good life is about more than status, job titles and climbing the greasy pole of career success. You're more interested in enjoying your time on this planet, in being laid-back and having fun. Or at least in making work as little of an inconvenience to the rest of your life as possible.

You don't need to be number one to feel good about yourself. Winning and coming out on top simply aren't that important. Others may need to be in charge, to put themselves forward and seek the limelight. They may chase the challenging projects and tough assignments, all the while hoping for the boss's job. You probably know people like that, who are willing to claw and fight, back-stab and do whatever it takes to get ahead. In meetings they talk purely for the sake of talking, to get noticed and score points. But that's not you.

You prefer to sit back and watch everyone else compete for attention, avoiding the office politics and dramas. You're happy to be a part of the team, to follow rather than lead and be content that your *real* life is outside of work.

Life is too short to spend it all at the office. Sure, you may want to be more successful – you wouldn't say no to a salary hike – but you're definitely not willing to sacrifice everything to get it.

The High-Drive person: striving, always aiming to achieve more

You have an unabashed need to achieve. You crave a direction, a destination, a target, something to focus your energies on. You set and accomplish goals. You push yourself to hit ambitious, sometimes scarily audacious goals. And the moment you think you're close to hitting a goal, you move the goalposts. You make it harder for yourself because you know you're capable of even more.

Given your gung-ho pace and kick-ass energy, you probably hate having nothing to do. You'd rather be busy and rushed off your feet than told to take it easy.

You don't push yourself for the fun of participating – you compete to win. You have high expectations and, deep down, you know that you don't want to settle for second place. While others may hate having their performance measured, you don't mind – you may even enjoy it. How can you tell how you're doing unless you're measured and can compare yourself to other people?

You find it especially maddening when people moan about a situation but aren't willing to do anything about it. When you're not happy, you take control. You take charge and you're pleased to tell others what they should be doing, how they can make a difference and contribute to the team. In fact, being in the driving seat is where you feel at your best. Truth is, you don't like being told what to do.

Neither do you believe in luck. Others may wait for an opportunity to come their way, to win big on the lottery or have that plum job fall into their lap. But you know that successful people make their own luck. You take the initiative, work hard and make things happen.

Make the most of yourself – for Low-Drive people

I can understand if you see your work as only one aspect of your life. You have family, friends and interests that you want to put first. But are you really happy or merely resigned to your lot in life?

Many of the Low-Drive people I meet feel at least occasionally that they're adrift in life. That they are merely going through the motions of life without accomplishing much. I don't want to presume that's you. But if you've ever wished you could take more control over your life and career, you're in the right place to discover how.

Take a cold hard look at your job

You probably have to work for a living, to put a roof over your head and food on the table. So let me ask you a question: How happy are you in your job? Do you see it as an interesting challenge or something to be endured?

You spend more of your waking hours at work than doing anything else. Even a fair amount of the time you spend at home seems to be about getting ready to go to work or trying to recover from bad days at work. But isn't life too short to put up with a job that you don't like that much?

Over to you

Take 30 seconds to note whether you agree or disagree with each of the following five statements:

- If I won the lottery, I definitely wouldn't carry on with the work I'm currently doing.
- All of my most significant achievements and memories happen outside of work.
- I often get that 'Monday morning feeling'.
- I frequently feel frustrated or bored with my work.
- If I could live my life over again, I wouldn't choose to do what I'm currently doing.

If you agreed with two or more of the above statements, you may need a sobering rethink about what you're doing. If you said 'Yes' to four or all five of these statements, then finding a new line of work should be a major priority.

Work shouldn't be a hardship to be endured. However, I've worked with some people who seem to be having a contest as to who is the most miserable about their work.

'I hate my job.'

'No, *I* hate mine more.'

'But *my* boss treats me really badly.'

'Oh, if you think that's bad, wait till you hear *this*.'

You probably know people like that. Perhaps they think it's cool to be cynical, negative and grumpy. To me it's a waste of a life. Surely it's better to change your circumstances than moan? To find a new job than settle for an awful one?

That's probably not you though. Perhaps you're more like the people I meet who put up with their work because they tell themselves, 'One day I'll do what I love – I just need to earn enough to put a deposit on a house/put the kids through university/pay off that loan . . .' Of course, you might keel over dead tomorrow. If you keep putting off the life you want to be living, you might never get there.

If you only had a year to live, would you go to work, doing the same job every day? Probably not. What if you only had five years to live? Suppose a doctor who has never been wrong tells you that you will drop dead in exactly five years' time. Would you carry on doing what you currently do? That's a tougher question, but perhaps you're thinking, 'Possibly not.' What if the doctor said that you have exactly ten years to live. What then?

Well, I can tell you for a fact that you will die. Hopefully not for many years, but there are no guarantees as to how much time any of us have on the planet. So why waste any more time doing something that you don't love?

Find your flow

Work doesn't have to be hard work. Some people discover work that they enjoy or even love. And when you love your work, you can't help but achieve and succeed.

'When you're in a job that you enjoy and you're good at, you're not just a better worker, you're a better spouse, a better parent, a better citizen,' advises Nooruddin 'Rudy' Karsan, CEO and boss of over 1000 employees at Kenexa, the human resources consultancy he founded.

So what do you love doing? What gets you stoked up, excited?

Psychologist Mihaly Czikszentmihalyi observes that people are happiest when they are completely engaged in the task that they're doing. When you immerse yourself in an activity so totally that you lose track of time, your brain suddenly fires on all cylinders. You feel carefree and alive. When you're completely absorbed in what you're doing, you experience a perfect moment that athletes call 'being in the zone' and which Czikszentmihalyi calls a state of 'flow'.

People experience flow in different ways. Perhaps you feel flow when you play a favourite sport, write computer code, dance to your favourite song, fix your car, complete a task, work in the garden. Or talk to your best buddy, repair a household appliance, play an instrument, write a letter, seal a business deal, make gifts for friends.

If you're lucky, you may already experience flow in some aspects of your work. A colleague gets into this state when he coaches people to solve their problems. A friend who works for an airline can chat quite effortlessly to passengers for hours. But many people have engaging and involving hobbies and interests that have little to do with their work. A client of mine who works in human resources gets the biggest buzz from tinkering around with components and building her own computers.

Another loses himself for hours reading design magazines or programming the features on his iPod and mobile phone.

When you find something that you love doing, you'll end up succeeding – quite by accident. I discovered ten years ago that I enjoyed writing. But I was working as a business analyst at the time, entering numbers into spreadsheets and cranking out the results. I had no opportunity to write more than a few sentences at a time, let alone a book. Still I knew that I wanted to write. I approached a publisher and persuaded them to let me write a slim book – barely bigger than a pamphlet really. When I got my first royalty cheque, I realised that I would have earned more per hour scrubbing toilets or washing dishes. But I didn't care – I loved writing. More than a dozen books later, my last book, *Confidence* (Prentice Hall, 2008) was chosen by WH Smith to be its August 'Book of the month'. Almost without intending to, I have succeeded – because I'm doing something that I love.

When you identify what you love to do, you'll succeed, without having to try. So let me ask you the question again: What do you *love* to do?

Over to you

Most people have quite a few different ways to get into a state of flow. Mihaly Czikszentmihalyi has asked thousands of people the question: 'Do you ever get involved in something so deeply that nothing else seems to matter and you lose track of time?' He's found that most flow experiences happen when people are actively engaged in a task rather than passively relaxing. People are three times more likely to experience flow when they're playing games and sports than watching television.

So now it's your turn. What do you do that makes you feel exhilarated, that makes you feel you're having a good day? What do you do for free – or for less than you'd get for cleaning toilets? Write down five of your favourite pursuits now.

- Play football
- Write my football blog
- Write history essay
- I'd teach history!
- ......

But don't stop there. Keep jotting down other activities. Over the coming weeks, note the moments when you feel a buzz or high – capture all the activities that make you feel that way.

Tweak, change, modify – or move on

Once you've identified the tasks and moments that help you to experience flow, think about how you could pursue work that allows you to experience more of it. Look for similarities between what you enjoy and what you *could* be doing at work. Ask your boss for assignments that allow you more moments of flow. Rather than wait for your boss to give you work that you don't enjoy, propose projects that not only benefit the organisation but also give you pleasure.

Look for ways to speed up or eliminate the dull bits of your job so you can linger on the tasks you like. Tell your colleagues what you enjoy most and volunteer when the right opportunities arise. See if you can swap duties with a colleague. For example, if someone doesn't like spreadsheets but you do, then offer to do her number crunching in exchange for something that you don't enjoy but she does. Or delegate if you have the luxury of a team or assistant to depend on.

Even if you can't change whole chunks of your work, look for small ways to tweak your job and create more moments that you enjoy. If one of your favourite flow activities is chatting to friends, see if you can spend more time talking to customers or colleagues in meetings. If you experience flow when playing computer games, ask for projects that allow you to immerse yourself in technology.

Another option is to look for a new job. Perhaps a move to a different team or department within your organisation. Or a switch to an entirely new kind of work elsewhere.

Over to you

Your personality should give you further powerful clues as to how you can experience flow.

If you're a High-Conscientiousness person, you may enjoy routine and getting to know the intricacies of your job in depth. If you're low on Conscientiousness, you may thrive on uncertainty and change. If you're a Low-Sensitivity person, you'll most enjoy environments where you can get straight to the point and speak your mind. But if you're a High-Sensitivity person, you would probably do better with colleagues who appreciate you for taking a subtler route.

Look back at the other six dimensions of personality. Try completing the following sentences:

- Considering my level of Inquisitiveness, I would be most fulfilled by pursuing work and personal situations that allow me to …
- Considering my level of Resilience, I would be most fulfilled by pursuing work and personal situations that allow me to …

Do the same for Affiliation, Conscientiousness, Sensitivity and Knowledge Questing. Just work through each personality dimension and try to identify a set of guiding principles for your career. Assemble a profile of the perfect work and environment for you.

I coach Mariel, the creative head at a large and prestigious advertising agency. When I first met her, she was in charge of a team of over 20 creative types. But when she wrote down all of the things that made her happy, that helped her to experience flow, she realised that managing people wasn't one of them. She most missed shooting and editing videos, being hands-on and doing the work that her team was doing. So she decided to quit her job to set up her own business. Moving away from managing a large team, she could get stuck into all of the tasks that made her come alive again.

Here's another example. Antoni Porras used to work as a sales and marketing manager for a technology company in Girona, Spain. But he had another passion: putting people in touch with other people. He couldn't find a job that allowed him to spend all of his time collaborating with other people, so he started his own business – a networking club. He puts people in touch with each other, acting as a broker for people who want to franchise their restaurant chain in the Middle East or find investors to launch a fashion line. He told me, 'Networking is my style of life, not just my work. I'm working for my dream.' With the dream has come success. Only two years after starting up his business, he is already running regular events in London, Barcelona and Dubai.

Get fired up – before you get fired

Perhaps you're thinking that having a job you enjoy is merely a nice-to-have rather than a must-have. But let's look at it another way. Organisations aren't known for their caring, sharing treatment of people. If your organisation were to restructure, who do you think they would keep – the people who seem at least a little motivated about their work or the ones who seem to be putting up with it?

Sorry to be blunt, but I want you to be clear: rekindling your motivation and having a job you enjoy isn't a luxury – it's a necessity.

Over to you

Here's another exercise that you can do very quickly. Peter Fennah, director of the career development service at Cranfield School of Management, suggests picking three friends who know you well. Give them a call and ask these three simple questions:

- 'How would you describe me?'
- 'What passions and interests do you think I have?'
- 'What could you see me doing and being good at?'

Don't butt in. Listen to their answers and write down their impressions of you. What themes or patterns emerge?

Follow your personal sat nav for success

Know any successful people? Probably. Take a moment to summon a few of them to mind.

Now, let me ask you: do any of them flail around, not knowing what they want from life? Do they sit around, waiting for opportunity to come their way? No, didn't think so.

Successful people have goals to strive for. They decide what they want and take steps to achieve it. They have a direction, a purpose, a vision. Only by having such a destination can they know whether they're making progress or not. Otherwise it's like getting into your car and deciding simply to follow the car in front. 'Well, I don't know where I want to go, so I'll do what everyone else seems to be doing.'

People who have a vision feel more fulfilled. You can do whatever you want, but you have to know what you want! You can use a picture of a bright, sunshiny future to motivate you through the here and now. Then, even when you're bogged down in a bad day, you can look forward to a better future. You can take comfort that a day's drudgery might be an important piece of that bigger picture.

Peter Fennah at Cranfield School of Management, one of the country's top business schools, tells me:

> *You can shape your life to make it more exciting. So many people go through life feeling that work is something that is done* to *them. But you can create your own dynamic, peppy environment. Work out an agenda, a goal, a target and then work towards it.*

Over to you

Deciding on a set of goals for life can be daunting, but here's a quick exercise to get you started.

Reflect on your life. Imagine that it's many years from now and you're reaching the end of your life. Looking back at the person you were and the things you did, complete these sentences.

- 'I am most proud of ....'
- 'I envy people who ....'
- 'I am glad that I put .... first.'
- 'I wish that I had done more of ....'

Honestly, bucketloads of research have proven that high achievers have goals in life. Successful people don't let their bosses and co-workers or family and friends dictate what they should be doing in their lives. They take charge. They identify what they want and set out to find or craft their perfect lives and careers.

Now it's your turn.

Become your best: Deciding what you want out of life

Find at least 15 to 20 minutes of time when you can sit and think. Write down what a successful and fulfilled life would look like for you in say five or ten years' time. Think about what you would like to be doing, what you'd like to be achieving and which people you'd like to be spending your time with.

It's your life, so it's up to you to decide what your goals are. So what do you want from life? Perhaps you want to be a successful entrepreneur or to get that corner office and chauffeur-driven car that come with being on the board of directors. To travel the world and experience as many different cultures as possible. To earn enough to retire at 50 or 40 or 30 – or perhaps to go on working until you're 80 because you love your work so much. To be a good parent or a devoted partner. To raise lots of money for charity or a cause that is dear to you.

Invest some time and thought in writing down what you'd love to have in your life and who you'd like to be. You'll thank yourself for it one day.

Put pen to paper – your future self will thank you for it

Have you written down your vision? If you have, well done. If you haven't, please, please go and do it. There's a big difference – *huge* difference – between understanding an idea and doing it. We all understand the point of getting fitter, but how many of us actually do it? The same goes for creating a vision. Of course you understand what it's about. But actually, the key to success comes from *doing,* not comprehending.

Once you've got your vision, you know what you want to achieve. Next, start scribbling down all the steps you must take to make it happen.

I coached a manager whose vision was to work as a vet. She needed to study to get A levels in biology and chemistry – doing it part-time took her two years. Plus, she needed to put aside enough money to take a further six years off to go to university – she's partway through her studies now. A daunting challenge to most people, but it's been her dream and she's making it happen.

Now is as good a time as any. So list all the actions you'll need to take to achieve your vision. Think about who you'll need to involve, what money you'll have to set aside, what training you may need. Consider which people to talk to for advice, which books to consult, what research to do. Scribble down every step that comes to mind. Some of the steps may be bigger than others, but just get it all down.

Then make a start. Pick an easy action from your list and do today what you could so very easily put off until tomorrow. Doesn't matter how small that action is – get started and you will soon build your momentum, creating your new future one step at a time.

Make the most of yourself – for High-Drive people

High-Drive people like you can be admired for taking the initiative. You're willing to push yourself to Herculean levels to get things done. You see even the biggest predicaments as challenges to be overcome rather than obstacles to be avoided. Your desire to win and get ahead means that you put in long hours and do whatever it takes to succeed. Perhaps you empathise with Michael Phelps, winner of eight gold medals at the Beijing Olympics, who said, 'I don't like to lose – not in swimming, not in Monopoly – *ever*.'

All of that's great when it comes to delivering on your promises. People know that they can give you a task and you'll complete it no matter what. But it can also cause problems. I work with many gifted, determined individuals – people who've been picked out of the crowd for their high potential. And I see a certain pattern over and over again: the problems come when you have to work with people who don't have the same levels of Drive.

You are happy to push yourself to heroic lengths and do whatever it takes, but not everyone else is happy to be pushed, to work as hard as you're willing to work. When a High-Drive person like you has to work with people who may be average or even low on Drive, *that's* when sparks may fly.

Delegate and coach, train and explain

Being a High-Drive person, you get things done much faster than most of the people you know. Why delegate a task to someone else when it's faster to do it yourself?

But imagine that a four-year-old boy – perhaps your son or nephew – comes to you, shoes in his tiny hands. He can't do his shoelaces up. Would you simply tie his shoelaces for him or try to teach him how to do it?

If you tie his shoelaces for him today, are you going to tie them tomorrow, and the next day, and the year after that? Imagine tying them for him, day in, day out, for the next dozen or more years.

Of course, it's ridiculous to think of an 18-year-old who can't tie his shoelaces. But say a member of your team comes to you with a problem. He doesn't know what to do and wants your opinion. You tell him how you'd handle it, sorting the situation out for your employee. He goes away happy, but what has he learned? Not a lot. If anything, he's learned that he can always rely on you to do his thinking for him.

That's the risk that comes with solving people's problems rather than giving them the skills and confidence to do it themselves.

Whether it's in the workplace or the home, you need to develop the people around you, to coach and guide them until they can do it as well as you.

Coach by telling people *what* you want rather than *how* you want it

You probably find it difficult to watch others perform tasks less effectively than you could yourself. But the trap of doing it all yourself is that you will always be overworked, overstretched and picking up the pieces. How can people ever learn and get better if you're always doing it for them?

Coaching people is essentially very straightforward. You don't need to read a hefty tome or go on a course to learn it. In fact, I would say that there's only one key principle: tell people *what* you want them to do rather than *how* to do it.

Say you want a colleague, Tanya, to arrange the annual Christmas dinner for the team. You could explain *what* you want her to achieve – to book a mid-priced restaurant that can seat 12 people on 15 December. Alternatively, you could explain *how* you want her to do it – to pick up the telephone directory and call at least 20 restaurants, asking them to fax their menus over.

Think about it though. In terms of *how* the task could be done, there are many ways to do it. She could search online instead of using a telephone directory. She could telephone friends for recommendations. Or she could send an email to all the members of the team, asking for ideas.

Over-eager managers often fall into the trap of telling people how the work should be done rather than what the work should achieve. They focus on the approach rather than the outcome. But by asking others to do a task the same way you do it, you cut off any chance of them finding an even better way to do it. You inadvertently force them to go through the motions, following instructions like a trained monkey, rather than engaging their brains.

Telling people *how* to achieve a task gives them insufficient freedom in terms of approach – you assume they're stupid and can't be trusted. Telling people *what* you want them to achieve gives them greater scope to use their initiative.

So whenever you want people to learn and grow, you need to concentrate on the results you want them to achieve, the outcome, the end goal, the finished result. Only then can they learn to think for themselves, become more confident and, ultimately, take some of the workload off your shoulders.

Ask more questions

Say you want a colleague to manage a large and complicated project, but he's stuck. He doesn't know where to begin. What then?

Telling people what you want them to achieve is a start. But if you walk away now, you're not coaching – you're merely dumping, leaving them up the proverbial creek without a paddle. Coaching means giving people the opportunity to think through how they might achieve the result you want. And that happens by asking questions.

When someone doesn't know what to do, you're probably dying to share your thoughts, to explain how you'd do it. Your best bet, however, is to ask questions:

- 'What have you considered so far?'
- 'What other options do you have?'
- 'Which option do you think would be the most effective?'
- 'Why?'

Your colleague may come up with the same solution that you would have suggested or a completely different one. Either way, it is his idea. He has a vested interest in making it succeed. He feels in control, empowered, responsible.

Just be sure to ask open-ended questions that make people think. Avoid closed questions that are merely statements with a question mark at the end, such as:

- 'Wouldn't it be better to do it like this?'
- 'Don't you think it would be stupid to do it that way?'
- 'Surely those numbers don't add up?'

If your question can be answered with a 'yes' or 'no', it's not an open-ended question – it's a statement posing (badly) as a question.

Anyone can give advice and tell people what to do. But taking the time to ask intelligent questions – that's something only the very best do. That's what you will do from now on too.

Unleash the potential of others through praise

High-Drive people like you are great at getting the job done, no matter what. When someone asks you to do something, you do it. You get on with it, no matter how much grief and hard work it entails.

Regrettably, not everyone is like you. The world would be a much more productive place if they were, but most people lack your level of determination, your grit and self-motivation.

I worked with someone I'll call Julian, a self-made mogul and co-owner of a chain of golf and leisure clubs. He had been sent to me for coaching by his business partner. His issue: he refused to praise anyone. He explained:

> *If I see a waitress has laid 39 tables in the dining room but forgotten one, she has failed to do her job. If I see that the groundskeeper has mown the lawn perfectly apart from even one small patch, that's not a job well done.*

He argued that the pay they received should be more than ample incentive to do a perfect job. I told him that he'd missed the point. I talked to his team members and they felt ignored, forgotten, neglected. He was depriving his employees, his suppliers and even his business partner of the emotional pay-off of doing good work.

Julian didn't want to give praise when he didn't believe that it was warranted. He said that he didn't want to pretend to be pleased when he wasn't. But I explained that wasn't what I was asking him to do. I wanted him to simply ignore the less-than-perfect results and praise the genuinely good results.

Surely there must be the occasional day when the waitress lays all of the dining room tables correctly? Tell her on those rare occasions that she's done a great job and she may do it again. With the groundskeeper, praise the areas that look beautiful. If the lawn outside reception looks great but the area out the back looks untidy, only mention how good the front looks.

Over several months, Julian conceded that it was paying off. Praising the occasional successes was encouraging his team to work harder. The business partner who had sent him for coaching also reported that the improvements in morale and productivity in the team were enormous.

People bring an enormous amount of discretionary effort to the work they do. Whether it's the cleaner who comes to your home once a week, your partner who makes dinner when you're too tired to cook or a colleague who covers for you in a meeting. They can go through the motions and do as little as they can get away with or put their hearts and souls into it. The difference? A few words of praise delivered sincerely.

Over to you

Here's a small experiment for you. Find something positive to say about the next few people you talk to and see what happens. The only condition is that you must only compliment something that you believe to be true.

Perhaps you meet a colleague and could drop into the conversation, 'By the way, I really did appreciate you looking over my draft report last week. I don't think I said how helpful it was.' Or you could tell a customer, 'I don't think I've ever mentioned that you're very laid-back and easy to work with.' Even tell a friend or loved one why you value them – for their support, brains, loyalty, humour, whatever.

What effect did it have on each person? And how little did it cost you?

Mike Kraus has managed people for over 15 years, in businesses ranging from retailers and design firms to the Walt Disney Company. Currently principal at StoreTouch Inc., he never underestimates the power of praise:

> *People go to work for an individual, not an organisation. Most employees look to gratify their managers like kids look to please their parents or teachers. You'd be hard pushed to overpraise.*

Science backs up the power of praise too. Researcher Paulette McCarty, at Northeastern University, asked a group of business school students to work on a creative problem-solving task. She gave a third of the students positive feedback, another third of the students negative feedback and the final third no feedback.

As you'd expect, positive feedback helped people to feel more positive about their efforts. However, receiving no feedback was as devastating to their self-confidence as receiving outright criticism.

To spell it out: most people find it as crushing to hear nothing about their performance as to be told off. So never assume that the people around you know they're doing a good job. Quite the opposite, they probably think that your silence means they're doing a bad job.

So stay quiet if you want people to believe the worst and let their performance slip. Praise sincerely if you want them to feel good and work hard. The choice is yours.

Become your best: Tapping into the power of praise

Even superstars need other people. Olympic athletes and sports stars rely on their coaches, sponsors, physiotherapists and nutritionists. Oscar-winning actors work with great directors, producers and co-stars. And your success is dependent on contributions from others too. It's time to recognise them and ensure they continue to contribute to your upward ascent.

As a High-Drive individual, you're probably used to working hard even when the praise isn't lavish and forthcoming. But remember that you're in the minority! You may enjoy praise, but many of the other people around you actually *need* words of genuine praise and sincere recognition to be at their best and work hard.

Make a list of the 10 or 20 people on whose contributions you most depend. If you're in charge of a team (as so many High-Drive people are), you should include every member of that team. Add in all of the people in other departments with whom you work closely – perhaps you rely on key people in finance for numbers or you liaise regularly with a couple of people in marketing or operations. Don't forget that loved ones and even a friend or two may provide you with invaluable support too – anything from cooking you a meal or picking up the kids to listening to your woes.

At the end of every day, glance through your list and consider whether or not you need to thank any of these people. Perhaps they did a great job, met a deadline, finished a project. Even if they didn't achieve a successful result, they may still have put in time and effort that deserves recognition. But only single them out if they genuinely did a good job.

Then say thank you. Do it face to face, one on one. You don't need a big speech, any fuss, flowers or champagne. Saying, 'Thank you for . . .' is usually quite enough. Perhaps a two-line email that starts, 'I didn't tell you the other day, but I wanted to thank you for . . .' Or occasionally, 'I don't tell you enough, but I want to mention how much I appreciate . . .'.

Show your appreciation. Be genuine. Be sincere.

Straightforward enough, right? Sounds like a complete no-brainer? It is, as long as you *do it*.

Many High-Drive individuals shy away from giving praise. They don't want to come across as fake by giving too much of it. That's rarely an issue, though. I'm sure you've heard people grumbling that people never say 'Thank you' or acknowledge the work they've done. But when was the last time you heard people complain they're sick of working for bosses who are too grateful for their hard work and efforts? That they're being appreciated or applauded *too much*?

Didn't think so.

Do the tombstone test

Hunger and ambition can have personal costs too.

I met a manager I'll call Matt at an assessment centre that I was running at an international bank. The bank employs hundreds of international executives (IEs) who act as an elite troubleshooting team. When a subsidiary of the bank is struggling anywhere in the world, the bank parachutes an IE in to sort it out. In his late twenties and already earning six figures, Matt was being evaluated for an even bigger promotion. He passed the gruelling tests at the assessment centre.

So why did the senior bosses at the bank turn him down?

They were concerned about his ability to sustain his pace. They discussed the fact that he worked *too* hard. He worked 16 or 18 hours a day, 6 or 7 days a week and had no personal life. His wife had divorced him. He had put his son into boarding school so he could take on international assignments. He had few friends outside of work.

So despite the fact that he was doing a great job, the big bosses decided not to promote him. He was already running at 99 per cent, unwilling or unable to slow down. He was burning through his body's fuel, close to running on empty. Would an even bigger job tip him over the edge?

When I gave Matt the bad news about the promotion, he was surprisingly composed. He said that he'd been thinking about his life recently anyway. On a flight, he had watched *The Bucket List*, starring Jack Nicholson and Morgan Freeman as two terminal patients who decide to make a list of everything they want to do in life before they 'kick the bucket'. Matt was almost grateful for his wake-up call.

Over to you

OK, *you* may be happy working long, hard hours. But here's another, perhaps more terrifying, way to look at your life. We never know how long we have with our loved ones. If your most cherished partner, friend, parent or child only had five years to live, how would you change your life?

Don't kill yourself working hard because you think that you're doing it for your loved ones. Don't assume you know what they want, that you can read their minds. Ask them and they may tell you they'd rather have you around than the material possessions your hard work is buying them.

So who are the three most important people in your life? Write their names down here.

- ....
- ....
- ....

Now go and ask them, 'How happy are you with our relationship? How could I make it better? To what extent is my workload an issue?'

Do it. Ask not only about the *quantity* of time you spend together but also the *quality*. If you don't ask them, is it because you're afraid they'll tell you something you don't want to hear?

Little in life is guaranteed, but I can promise you this: you will die. No one on their deathbed ever said, 'I wish I'd spent more time at the office.' Or, 'Hey, at least I got good performance reviews.' What would *you* say in your final moments?

Some High-Drive people prefer to disregard such thoughts. They live in the moment and want to ignore the inevitable. But they're often the ones who succumb most spectacularly to a midlife crisis.

Buying a sports car, dressing like a teenager, having an affair and taking up a dangerous sport – all of those are often desperate attempts by people caught in midlife crises to find meaning in their lives. Don't let that be you.

Become your best: Living for the here and now

Although it's admirable that you have goals, don't let them dominate your life. The risk of being too goal-driven is that you keep deferring the rest of your life in the pursuit of those goals.

Instead, think about the end of your life, then work backwards. Assume that you have lived to the ripe old age of 100. (With modern medicine, that's becoming more and more likely.) Imagine you're on your deathbed. You'll find that your colleagues from wherever you work now won't be there. Do you honestly believe that your current boss will be such a close friend that he or she will be there with you saying a tearful goodbye? I don't think so. You'll be surrounded by family and friends.

How would you like them to remember you? What would you like them to say to you in your final moments? That you were a loving partner, a caring friend, a doting parent? Or that you were a driven boss, a rich entrepreneur, a merciless mogul?

Set aside the time to project yourself into the future and see your life from a fresh vantage point. Write down how you'd like to be remembered. Yes, actually write it out. Then read, review and rewrite it until it captures your definition of a successful and well-lived life.

Now think about what you can do today and every day to ensure that's how you'll be remembered. Avoid putting your life on hold until you attain the next goal or the one after that. Look for ways to appreciate what you already have rather than chase endlessly what you don't have. Don't wait until tomorrow to enjoy your life.

Actor, entrepreneur and philanthropist Paul Newman (he gave over $250 million to charity made from sales of his Newman's Own salad dressings) once said in an interview, 'Life is whimsical. Longevity is an incredible gift, and some people don't get to enjoy it.'

I hope that you have a long life, but more than that, I hope you enjoy it.

ONWARDS AND UPWARDS

Drive reflects people's natural desire to take charge, get ahead and achieve. Some people thirst for success. Others are more laid-back about it. Here's a summary of how the two ends of the range broadly differ.

Low-Drive	High-Drive
Tend to be laid-back, unassuming.	Tend to be determined, ambitious.
Happy to follow, let others take charge.	Prefer to be in charge, the boss, the leader.
Tend to put up with their circumstances.	Tend to want to change their circumstances.
Enjoy living for the moment, in the present.	Enjoy setting and achieving difficult goals.
Could come across as lazy or uncaring.	Could come across as pushy or intimidating.
Could perhaps push self harder.	May push themselves too much, work too hard.

If you scored lower on Drive:

- Recognise the nature of your personality. Avoid situations and organisations in which you are expected to compete and clamber over other people to get to the top. Don't try to be something you're not.
- Be careful not to settle for a job or any other situation that isn't good enough. Rather than just accept what you've got, why not decide what you want?
- Spend some time identifying the passions in your life, the stuff you enjoy doing so much that you lose track of time. Then look

for ways to blend your passions with your work – either in your current job or a new one.

- Invest a little time in creating a vision of the ideal life you'd like to be leading. No matter how daunting it may seem, you can make progress by taking even small steps, one day at a time.

If you scored higher on Drive:

- To achieve personal fulfilment and career success, recognise that you feel at your best when you are given clear feedback on your performance, how you're doing and what you could be doing better.
- Realise that leaders only succeed by building both the skills and confidence of their teams. Resist the urge to take everything on yourself. Delegate tasks and coach people so that they can take on more responsibility.
- Learn that you are in the minority of people who are willing to work hard no matter what. Other people's willingness to work hard can depend on how much praise and recognition they receive. Remember, few people complain that they're appreciated too much.
- Consider that few people in their latter years wish they'd worked harder. Of course your work is a big part of who you are. But don't focus so intently on your career that you neglect the rest of your life.

09

Taking yourself to the next level

"A good plan vigorously executed right now is far better than a perfect plan executed next week."

George Patton, US general

Your personality is as unique as a snowflake. Perhaps you're ultra-high or super-low or somewhere in between on each dimension. Whatever your pattern, you should now understand the profound nature of your personality. You should have a good idea of your strengths and shortcomings, the situations that suit you and those that don't.

Now what?

In this chapter, I'll walk you through five simple steps to create your personal action plan. You can find fulfilment and achieve your goals.

Step 1: Find a niche but take responsibility for change

You have a unique personality, a set of preferences that governs how you think and feel. You must respect this individual nature. You will be most fulfilled by pursuing work and personal situations that allow you to deploy your strengths. Rather than fighting constantly against your natural inclinations, recognise that certain pathways and life choices suit you better than others.

If you find certain tasks at work either mind-numbingly boring or heart-stoppingly stressful, try to swap them with a colleague who is excited by them. If you hate particular chores at home, offer to do something else useful instead. Say 'yes' to what suits you; where possible, politely turn down what doesn't. Pursue opportunities that feel right and get out of bad routines. Even change jobs, find new friends.

Listen to the authentic voice within you that is your personality. And use all of the talents you have at your disposal to make your situation fit you – not the other way around. This is about finding a niche that allows you to be comfortable, happy, fulfilled.

When you play to your strengths you can't help but do well. Success becomes the happy accident of being in a situation that you enjoy. So every time you make a major decision about your life or your loves, your work or your home, ask yourself, 'Does this new situation allow me to be myself *most* of the time?'

Playing to your strengths, however, does *not* mean that you can excuse all of your flaws. No one can succeed by giving in to their instincts *all* of the time. Make no mistake, we all have habits that we could improve and change.

I sometimes hear people say they don't believe they can change. You probably know a few individuals like that too. They say things like:

- 'I've *always* had a quick temper.
- 'I *can't help* being negative.'
- 'I'm *too old* to change my ways.'
- 'I know I'm shy – *that's just the way I am*.'

They argue that their failings are down to their genetic make-up or perhaps the way they were brought up as children.

But they're wrong.

I like chocolate. My brain is somehow wired to give me a huge buzz whenever I wolf down a single piece. And then I want more, more, more. All the same, I can choose to pick up an apple instead of a chocolate bar.

Your brain's autopilot may be set to seek out order, precision and tidiness (or to hate it). But you can *choose* to be different. To relax your standards rather than come across as an uptight parent or micro-managing boss. Or tighten them up so you don't come across as sloppy and haphazard.

Remember, our brains continue to grow new brain cells right through to old age. I mentioned this in Chapter 1 but it's so important I'll say it again. We *can* learn new ways to behave. We *can* change our habits. We can learn to be less temperamental, more positive, more organised, more creative, less pushy and so on.

I'm sure you won't use such excuses to justify your behaviour. You won't use that kind of defeatist language – you know better. But it's worth mentioning if you ever decide to pass this book on to a colleague, a friend, a loved one. If you want other people to change, you have to help them understand that they must take personal responsibility for change.

Step 2: Decide on your priorities

I've presented you with plenty of ideas on how to develop yourself. Whether you're high or low or in between for each personality dimension, each chapter has given you a handful of recommendations on how to make the best of yourself.

Trouble is, seven personality dimensions multiplied by three or four recommendations each is a lot to take in all at once. So let's make it easier for you. Let's prioritise what you should be focusing on.

To start with, let's create a summary of your personality profile here. Copy out and complete the table opposite.

Most people find that it's the extremes of their personality that deserve the most attention. If you have a personality score for any particular dimension that is somewhere in the middle, that implies you have a balanced approach. Someone who is average for Inquisitiveness may be somewhat creative but also OK with implementation. Someone who's average for Sensitivity may be reasonably tactful yet also able to be direct when necessary. So for the moment, I suggest you ignore the personality dimensions where you score in the average zone.

Personality dimension	**Your score (low, average, high)**	**Possible actions to take to develop on this personality dimension**
Inquisitiveness		
Resilience		
Affiliation		
Conscientiousness		
Sensitivity		
Knowledge Questing		
Drive		

Step 3: Get a second opinion

This is optional, but I think you'll miss out if you don't do it.

When it comes to my personal development, I know I can always turn to David. I worked with David some years ago. We shared an office and had similar views about the world. We grumbled about the same things, got each other through tough times and had a laugh along the way. As well as being a good friend, he's bright and always has an opinion. He has my best interests at heart and I trust him to tell me the truth. Even if the truth is hard-hitting and something I don't necessarily want to hear.

So who would your David be?

Before you decide what you should do to develop yourself, get a second opinion from your David. You're looking for someone who:

- knows you well

- wants you to succeed and has your best interests at heart
- will tell you the truth about yourself.

Show the table you created in Step 2 to your David. Explain each of the personality dimensions and what your scores are. Explain that you want to get better at everything you do and ask, 'Which of these actions do you think would make the biggest difference to me?'

Ask the question, then listen to the answers. Be prepared for an interesting conversation!

Step 4: Choose your top three

Time to choose what you're going to do. Taking into consideration your own thoughts and the second opinion you've been given, what do *you* think you need to work on most?

Think about what people say to you. Does your partner wish that you could be more outgoing or more retiring? Does your boss criticise you for being insufficiently creative or so inspired that you never finish anything off? Do you wish deep down that you could be more of something or less of something else?

Look back at your table from Step 2 and at what you put in the column of possible actions to take. Looking only at those personality dimensions where your scores were either high or low, ask yourself, 'Which handful of actions jump out at me?' Which three to five actions strike you as having the potential to make the biggest difference to your life, work, satisfaction and success?

Write at least three (but no more than five) actions out here:

- Action 1: ....
- Action 2: ....
- Action 3: ....

Don't worry. We're not going to ignore all of the other development actions that you could be taking. But it's good to start with a small number. Once you've gained momentum and made progress with this initial handful, you can come back and add more actions to your list.

Step 5: Set goals so that you can score

Perhaps you know someone who joined a gym but gave up? Or someone who decided to give up cigarettes or chocolate or some other vice but who ultimately couldn't manage it? Well, that's not going to happen to you.

Having the ambition to change is a great start. But research tells us that people with vague, insufficiently focused goals nearly always fall back into old habits. Whether you believe in the power of cosmic ordering or the psychology of goal-setting, I can tell you that you will achieve more by setting decisive goals.

Four letters make all the difference: SPOT. These will help us because we have the best shot of changing our behaviour when we set goals that are:

- **S**tretching and significant
- **P**ositive
- **O**bservable
- **T**imed

I have written a lot about the psychology of goal-setting in another book, *Confidence: The art of getting whatever you want* (Prentice Hall, 2008), but I'll summarise it for you here.

Your goals need to have the following qualities:

- **Stretching and significant.** Your goals have to be at least a little challenging and motivating. You have to *want* to change. If you're changing purely because someone else is nagging you, you won't have the motivation to keep it up. So only choose goals that you *really*, *really* want.

- **Positive.** The brain works in mysterious ways. One odd fact is that the brain struggles to deal in negatives – 'Don't eat a burger', 'Don't get angry', 'Stop being so shy'. When we hear instructions like those, we tend to ignore the 'don't' or 'stop' and instead focus on 'burger', 'angry', 'shy' so we actually make ourselves *more* likely to want a burger, get angry or be shy! So avoid the word 'don't'. Instead focus on what you *do* want to do – 'Eat more salads', 'Stay calm', 'Speak up in public'. Lab studies tell us that people who set positive goals are more likely to achieve them. Enough said.
- **Observable.** Sportspeople have known this for years. When they practise, they set precise goals that third parties could observe and say, 'Yes, you did it' or 'No, that was no good.' When Tiger Woods hones his golf game, he doesn't say, 'I want to get better at golf.' No, he sets an observable goal, such as, 'I want to be able to hit a golf ball with a seven iron and get it to within ten feet of the hole 90 per cent of the time.' Only that way can you and any observers watch and say, 'Yes, you made it.' Make *your* goals observable and you will know when you've achieved them.
- **Timed.** Having a goal is great, but *when* are you going to do it? A big risk for lots of people is that they keep putting things off until tomorrow. But we all know that tomorrow never comes! Some people have the best intentions in the world, but never get started. They want to write a book, travel somewhere exotic, learn a language, take up a sport, chase a promotion, get a new job. But they say 'some day' afterwards and never get around to it. So set yourself a deadline. If you want to do something, put a big circle around the date in your diary, a big cross on your wall calendar. Tell colleagues or friends that you're

going to do it by 1 January next year or your birthday or your wedding anniversary. If it's work-related, tell your boss that you're going to do something by the end of the month, the next pay review, the next performance appraisal. Set a date and you'll have to get it done.

Here are some examples of SPOT goals people have set themselves:

- 'I will run a two-hour brainstorming session every quarter, starting at our away-day in June' (for a Low-Inquisitiveness person).
- 'I will ask for and gain written feedback from at least ten people by the end of this month' (for a High-Resilience individual).
- 'I will initiate contact and meet up with a colleague from another department for at least one coffee or lunch three days a week for the next month' (for a Low-Affiliation person).
- 'I will thank or praise or otherwise show my appreciation for at least one person every day. I will do this by speaking to someone face to face whenever possible' (for a High-Drive person).

You get the idea. So let's turn *your* top actions into SPOT goals. Rewrite them so that they're specific and significant, positive, observable and timed.

- SPOT goal 1: ....
- SPOT goal 2: ....
- SPOT goal 3: ....

ONWARDS AND UPWARDS

Congratulations! You're on your way. You're going to make the best of yourself. Now get out there and turn your actions into reality. Implement vigorously. Intentions are good, but doing is better.

You don't lose weight by just reading a book on diet and exercise, you have to apply it. Same goes for this book. You now understand how to manage your personality, but *you* have to make it happen.

Change your behaviour on a daily basis, as many times as you can. If you keep repeating your actions, they eventually become second nature. Keep going and then keep going some more.

And once you've explored your own personality and mastered your distinctive assets? The journey doesn't stop there. Think about the personality profiles of the people you work with or your loved ones. If you run a team, tailor your approach to capitalise on their individual strengths and you'll watch them come alive and reach dizzying heights. Use the seven dimensions to understand how people think, what makes them tick, why you may sometimes clash and how to get the best out of them.

Remember, I'm a psychologist – I do this leadership coaching and high achievement stuff for a living. I see how individuals who understand and refine the dimensions of their personalities go to work with a grin on their faces and can't help but succeed. I work with entire teams of people who learn the best ways to come together, play to their strengths and achieve their goals. So I know that *you* can make the best of yourself and the people around you too. This is your chance to learn, grow, improve and succeed. You can do it.